SCADA Security
What's broken and how to fix it

SCADA Security
What's broken and how to fix it

Andrew Ginter

www.scada-security.ca

 ABTERRA

Abterra Technologies Inc.

Calgary

SCADA Security – What's broken and how to fix it
Copyright © 2016 by Abterra Technologies Inc. All rights reserved.

WARNING

Published by Abterra Technologies Inc.
Calgary, Alberta, Canada
www.abterra.ca

ISBN 978-0-9952984-0-8 (softcover)
Fourth printing

To my parents Josef and Barbara,
who by their example
teach how to work, live, and love

Contents

Forward

Cybersecurity is the topic of the day and will remain so for years to come. IT organizations throughout the world struggle to protect their data, information, and intellectual property stored on Internet-connected networks. Software vulnerabilities are omnipresent with vendors providing constant security/patch updates. Antivirus providers cannot keep up and generally only catch attacks that are already in the wild. Firewalls are deployed everywhere, but few companies escape a damaging intruder penetration because it is so easy for an adversary to gain a foothold within the IT network and pivot to items of value. Losses easily total in the billions.

In the U.S., the President has delineated critical infrastructure sectors in the Presidential Policy Directive on Critical Infrastructure Security and Resilience. Not surprisingly, many of the sectors named fall into the category of Industrial Control Systems (ICS) – where operating machinery controlled by software is at the heart of the production process. SCADA systems control these processes. Successful attacks on ICS systems can lead to loss of production, unrecoverable damage to vital equipment, and even loss of life. If production in critical industries stops for even a few short weeks, our way of life begins to change in unthinkable ways. Yet, are these control systems any better protected than the IT systems that are so easily penetrated by attackers?

Across the globe, standards have arisen that attempt to address the increased need for security in the ICS world, but everywhere these standards are timeworn when enacted, while various groups of attackers sharpen their skills on a daily basis. The practice of cyber security means doing what is needed to protect ourselves adequately from attacks. Compliance with standards means doing what someone else has told us to do, whether it is useful or not. Standards are helpful but are ultimately a losing battle when compared to a strategy of constantly considering and enacting current best practices.

In this book, Mr. Ginter provides a thoughtful, coherent and thorough discussion of these matters. But he does not stop there. Uniquely, he proceeds to lay out a security architecture that will protect ICS systems with a much higher level of surety than approaches in common use today. Even beyond that, he outlines how the recommended architecture will be resilient given the inevitable trend toward greater digitization of ICS components, and the evolution of attackers.

Some will argue with the architecture or items in the treatment of all things cyber that lead to his conclusions. These arguments can only help the entire industry, as ICS organizations throughout the world struggle to find a sustainable path forward. I hope that many will see the wisdom in this book's discussion and recommendations, and will begin to implement those recommendations, thereby frustrating attackers by cutting off their attack loops and making them blind to the workings of our ICS software.

Finally, the readability of the book is noteworthy. A Board Director, CEO, CIO, CISO, or Security Architect can all read the book, which unravels like a detective story and is just as addictive. Reading a draft, I was unable to put it down as one chapter led to the next and today's myths and vulnerabilities were openly disclosed, leading ultimately to workable solutions that can and should be implemented today. It will take years for standards to catch up to this book, but best practice pursuers can pay attention today. For our way of life, I hope they do.

- - Paul Feldman, Energy Board Member and Advisor, Midcontinent ISO, Energy Sector Security Consortium, AMP Electrical, and others

Acknowledgements

No one lives or writes in a vacuum and I have been blessed with opportunity to hear and argue with a great many SCADA security experts over the course of many years. I extend special thanks to Lior Frenkel, CEO and Co-Founder of Waterfall Security Solutions. Lior is a fountain of ideas, which I have sampled and adapted in this work. Special thanks also to Paul Feldman, who helped me to understand board-level business drivers and decision-making, and whose early feedback very much improved the readability and relevance of this work.

I also thank my dedicated reviewers for their very valuable feedback: Lior Frenkel, Paul Feldman, Dr. Arthur Conklin, Dr. Chee-Wooi Ten, Andrea Ginter, Rachel Ginter, Betty Wong and Courtney Schneider.

Last and not least, I thank Betty, Andrea and Rachel again, for their encouragement and support, and for putting up with me slacking off on chores and other duties for these last 5 months that I have been pre-occupied with writing.

For the record, while I am grateful to everyone who has contributed to this book and to my understanding of these issues, no reader should assume that any of these good people agree with anything I have written. In fact, most of them have expressed disagreement with at least some of the points I make. The contents of this work express my own opinions, and not necessarily those of anybody else.

SCADA Security

"What do such machines really do?
They increase the number of things
we can do without thinking.
Things we do without thinking -
there's the real danger."

-- Frank Herbert, Dune, 1965

Chapter 1 – Introduction

Much has been written about the SCADA Security Problem – the risk that some cyber attack will shut down important industrial processes, cripple critical infrastructure, or cause an environmental disaster. The threat is real. The problem is that most of what has been written is either subtly or grossly wrong, and some is utter nonsense.

The first generation of SCADA security advice, published roughly 2003-2011, is subtly wrong. The defense-in-depth posture this advice advocates is costly, is often itself a threat to industrial safety and reliability, and fails to protect SCADA systems against modern attacks.

Most of this failed first-generation, defense-in-depth SCADA security advice is based on IT security principles. IT security principles fail to protect IT networks – all such networks are regarded by IT experts as essentially, constantly compromised. Intrusion detection and practiced incident response teams are considered best practices by IT experts. Response teams constantly seek to identify compromised computers, erase them, and restore them from backups. The essential problem with applying IT security principles to SCADA systems is this: there is no way to restore lost production, damaged turbines, or human lives "from backups."

It is therefore not surprising that the state of SCADA security is, on average, poor to atrocious in the vast majority of highly-computerized industrial sites all over the world.

In this book, we outline what is emerging as a new way of understanding SCADA security, and is increasingly reflected in modern advice published since about 2010. Preventing compromise of our SCADA systems and misoperation of our physical processes must be the priority, not detecting and remediating intrusions after the damage is done. Physical and network perimeter protections are the essential, primary protections in this new approach. Costly IT security measures with limited

1

effectiveness, including security update programs, encryption and intrusion detection systems, should all be secondary measures, addressing only residual risks. We can and should control our investment in these secondary measures to reflect their limited effects in terms of risk reductions.

IT experts will tell us this book is hopelessly ill-conceived. They are wrong. Anyone who works every day in the kill-zone of an "industrial incident" has a real, personal interest in deploying the strongest, practical, protective measures for SCADA systems. Everyone who is exposed every day to industrial risks is the focus for this book. We hope to provide enough information here to make the case for effective SCADA security systems, to protect our industrial practitioners from cyber attacks, and to protect all of us by keeping our essential industries running reliably in an increasingly connected, and increasingly hostile world.

Terminology

Please note that we may not define every technical term before using it. Readers not familiar with SCADA security terminology may wish to refer occasionally to the Glossary at the end of this text.

"Three laws of robotics:

(1) A robot may not injure a human being or, through inaction, allow a human being to come to harm.

(2) A robot must obey the orders given it by human beings except where such orders would conflict with the first law.

(3) A robot must protect its own existence as long as such protection does not conflict with the First or Second Laws."

-- Isaac Asimov, I, Robot, 1950

Chapter 2 – SCADA Security

To understand SCADA security, we must understand something about both SCADA systems and cyber security. We begin with SCADA systems.

SCADA Systems

SCADA systems are the computers that control important, complex, and often dangerous physical processes, many of which constitute the physical infrastructure critical to modern societies. These physical processes are powerful tools, and their misuse generally has unacceptable consequences. Preventing such misuse is the goal of SCADA security. To understand misuse and how to prevent it, we need some understanding of what a SCADA system is, and how it works.

Where to start? Industrial control systems are old – people were controlling physical processes with dials and gauges before there were computers, and have been using computers to assist with such control almost since the first computers were invented. As with any old field, the terminology is arcane. What the press calls a "SCADA system" is a misnomer.

Technically, "SCADA" stands for "Supervisory Control and Data Acquisition." A SCADA system is an industrial control system that spans a wide-area network (WAN) over long distances. Electric grids, pipelines and water distribution systems use SCADA systems. In contrast, "DCS" stands for "Distributed Control System." A DCS is an industrial control system where no WAN is involved, and the entire physical process is

3

contained in one comparatively small site. Power plants, refineries and chemical plants use DCSs. Historically, SCADA systems and DCSs were different – one kind of software could not control the other kind of process. Nowadays, general-purpose control system software has all of the features of both SCADA systems and DCSs, so the difference between the two terms is more usage than technology. The modern term encompassing DCSs, SCADA systems and all other kinds of control systems is "industrial control system" (ICS).

This means that, technically, the title of this book should be "Industrial Control System Security" not "SCADA Security." However, since many in the audience for this text are non-technical business decision-makers, we use the terms "SCADA security," "ICS security" and "control system security" largely interchangeably, as does the mass media.

Industrial processes can be subdivided as well. Most critical infrastructures are examples of "process industries." In process industries, the material being manipulated is more or less "goo" at some point in the physical process: water purification systems manipulate water, refineries manipulate oil, and pipelines move fluids. Electric grids are considered process industries as well, because electricity is produced in a continuous stream that can be modelled as more or less a fluid[1]. Even railway and traffic control systems are considered process systems, though this pushes the concept just a bit. Within process industries, there are batch industries and continuous industries. Batch industries, such as refining and pharmaceuticals, are industries where the production line does not run continuously. Instead, it produces identifiable batches of outputs. Continuous industries, such as water treatment plants, power plants and offshore oil production platforms, consume inputs and produce outputs more or less constantly.

Discrete manufacturing is the opposite of process industries. While process industries work with continuous inputs, discrete manufacturing assembles small, discrete components into larger outputs, such as automobiles, aircraft, and home appliances. There are many similarities between process and discrete manufacturing, but there are significant differences as well. For example, when a control system in a process plant

---

[1] Kirchhoff's first law states that electric currents flowing in a power grid have similar properties to incompressible fluids in a network of pipelines.

is sabotaged and the physical process is misoperated, there is often a real risk to human life at the plant and to the safety of the public in the immediate vicinity. When a control system in a discrete manufacturing plant is sabotaged, there can be a risk to any human operator working close to the affected machines or robots, but there is generally no immediate public safety risk. In both cases though, there is a real risk that the physical industrial process will be shut down as a protective measure. Such shutdowns are always costly to the business operating the industrial process, and can have societal consequences when the physical process constitutes a critical infrastructure.

Most of the examples in this book are about control systems in process industries, not discrete manufacturing. Cyber-security issues in the two domains are similar though, differing more in degree than in kind.

An important aspect common to all SCADA systems is the human operator. Control systems at important industrial facilities almost always have one or more human operators charged with ensuring the safe and reliable operation of the physical process. These operators use tools known as "human-machine interface" (HMI) software. This software almost always includes a graphical visualization of the state of the physical process, and often includes other elements such as alarm managers and historical trending tools.

By policy and sometimes by law, these operators are required to permit the physical process to operate only if they have a high degree of confidence that the process is operating safely. If the operator ever loses such confidence, for example because their displays freeze, or a message pops up saying "you have been hacked," they must take action. An affected operator may transfer control of the process to a secondary or redundant HMI or control system. If however, after some seconds or minutes, the operator is still not sufficiently confident of the correct and safe operation of the physical process, that operator, most often, must trigger a shutdown of the physical process.

This means that most often, the simplest way for an attacker to cause physical consequences is to impair the operation of some part of an operator's HMI or the systems supporting the HMI. The simplest physical consequences of such attacks are shutdowns of the physical process. Many industrial processes can be shut down much faster than they start up, and can take days to recover full production again after an emergency shutdown. In some cases, regulatory approvals must be obtained before restarting physical processes, delaying plant restarts by as much as months. Worse, emergency shutdowns can often put physical stress on industrial equipment, leading to immediate equipment failures or premature equipment aging.

IT/OT Integration

An important trend in SCADA systems since roughly the mid-1990's is what the Gartner Group has coined "IT/OT integration" [1]. The "IT" is of course information technologies and "OT" is "operations technologies" or more colloquially, SCADA systems. The IT/OT integration trend is towards integrated IT and OT teams, business processes, products, technologies and networks.

The Gartner group argued successfully that since both SCADA / OT and IT networks increasingly use the same computing hardware, operating systems, platform applications and networking components, there are cost savings and other benefits to merging these technology teams, application platforms, networks and business practices. Why, for example, would it make any sense to use one relational database vendor's product in a SCADA network when the business had already purchased an enterprise-wide license to deploy a different vendor's databases?

The problem with naïve IT/OT integration though, is that when the same technology is used on IT and SCADA networks, and when IT and SCADA networks are thoroughly interconnected, many of the same cyber attacks that succeed on IT networks succeed on SCADA networks.

Cyber Security

Cyber security is focused on preventing such attacks. SCADA security is focused on preventing any unauthorized operation of SCADA system computers. SCADA security is a more recent discipline than SCADA systems or automation systems, but is no less confusing. Newcomers to the security field see a bewildering variety of types of vulnerabilities, attacks, and defensive systems. Combine this with the perennial admonition that "a chain is only as strong as its weakest link" and the task of defending control systems can seem insurmountable.

This bewildering variety is an illusion. All vulnerabilities in software and indeed in systems of hardware, software and networks, are bugs or defects. The bewildering variety is simply the result of people trying to classify somehow, all possible defects – all the possible ways people can produce software and systems incorrectly. All such classification systems are doomed to fail – people can make mistakes in an uncountable number of ways.

This perspective simplifies much "security research" as well. When the only results of such "research" are new vulnerabilities in existing software products, this research is no more than post-product-release quality assurance (QA). To be fair, not all security research produces QA-like results. For example, the most useful research into vulnerabilities identifies entirely new kinds of vulnerabilities that nobody had before considered, and that all product developers must now start to consider and avoid.

Research into defensive techniques, their application and their effectiveness is of course also much more than QA. However, the vast majority of previously-undiscovered "zero day" vulnerabilities and exploits revealed at events such as the annual Black Hat conference are no more than new security defects discovered by unpaid post-release QA "security researchers."

Three Laws of SCADA Security

In hopes of simplifying the field of cyber security to the point where SCADA practitioners can make sense of and routinely apply sound security practices, we propose three laws of SCADA security. Yes, in modern times, scientists prefer the terms "principle" and "theory" to "law," but we are trying to simplify things here. These laws address fundamental cyber-security concepts that are poorly understood, and poorly communicated.

1) Nothing is secure

Security is a continuum, not a binary value. Given enough time, money and talent, any security posture can be breached. Anyone using terms such as "secure communications," "secure boot" or "secure operating system" is either selling something, or has just been sold a bill of goods.

This is important. It changes the conversation from "never you mind, I have security covered" to "just how secure are we?" and ultimately "how secure should we really be?"

7

2) *All software can be hacked*

All software has bugs. Software development teams work hard to eliminate what bugs they can, but in spite of their best efforts, essentially all software has bugs, even security software. Some bugs result in exploitable security vulnerabilities. For evidence of this, simply look at the support section of any software vendor's website and see how many security updates have been issued recently. In practice then, all software can be hacked[2].

This is important. Too many of us believe that patching known bugs and vulnerabilities makes us invulnerable. Others believe that the way to make software systems "secure" is to deploy more security software. This is all nonsense – there are vulnerabilities to be found in any software system, even security software.

3) *Every piece of information can be an attack*

Even a single bit of information – a one or a zero – can be an attack. If a plant operator is trying to turn off a piece of equipment with a zero, but an attacker changes that zero to a one, that is an attack. Passwords and malicious intent carried in the brains of people entering a plant can be an attack. Malware installed on brand new computers, or in the tiniest of computers embedded in USB keyboards, can be an attack.

---

[2] Some experts dispute this. For example, some academics claim that software can be proven correct. We remind them of the SSH protocol that was proven correct [56] and later defeated [55]. There is no known way to prove the movement of every quantum electron in a physical CPU chip, not by a huge margin. All proofs of correctness therefore are based on axioms that vastly simplify the physical world. This means such proofs can be vulnerable to attacks at lower levels of detail than the axioms at the foundation of the proof. Other purists argue that specific, widely-cited examples such as the TeX type setting language prove that defect-free and vulnerability-free software is possible. Still others point out that very small, heavily-reviewed, individual software components are arguably free of defects and vulnerabilities. We argue that defect / vulnerability insertion into products during software development and maintenance is a chaotic process, and reasonably random. After all, if the process were not random, we would be able to write programs to predict the locations of our bugs. The more code in the software product then, the greater the likelihood of defects and vulnerabilities. Modern software products, including SCADA systems and cyber-security systems, tend to be very large. Again, for evidence of vulnerabilities, simply visit a favorite vendor's website and look for published security updates.

More specifically, every communications message, whether Internet Protocol (IP), old-style RS-232 serial communications, or any other message always contains some sort of information, and can therefore be an attack. The Internet moves information in wholesale quantities. This makes the Internet a great enabler. It makes life so much more convenient for all of us and for our attackers as well.

Every message to any computer is also a kind of control. A computer receiving a message is executing code that the computer would not have executed without the message, and has thus been controlled to some extent by the message. Malformed messages are obvious attacks. Legitimate-seeming messages faking credentials are less obvious. Legitimate-seeming messages misusing legitimate credentials to control processes incorrectly are even harder to spot.

This is important. A compromised machine can be used to send messages to other machines and so attack machines deeper into a protected network or system of networks – this is called "pivoting" an attack. Any computer or device reachable directly or indirectly from the Internet via a path of pivoting through intermediate computers and communications links is at risk of sabotage from the Internet. This includes safety systems and equipment protection systems that are connected, directly or indirectly, to networked machines.

Putting the Pieces Together

Misoperation of industrial processes can have costly or even dangerous outcomes. For example, misoperation of the human-machine interface (HMI) for the SCADA system at British Petroleum's Texas City refinery in 2005 caused an explosion that killed 15 people, injured 180, shut the refinery down for one year, and cost BP one billion dollars in various kinds of damages [2]. Note that this was not a deliberate cyber attack, but misoperation of the HMI by the plant operator in violation of a number of BP's standing policies.

The essence of a SCADA security compromise is this: any operation that a human operator, such as the Texas City refinery operator, can legitimately instruct an HMI to carry out, an attacker with control of the SCADA system can also instruct the SCADA system to carry out. Although many safeguards are built into HMI and other control-system software components that prevent the operator from instructing the

9

physical process to enter dangerous states, an attacker who has compromised these software components can often bypass the safeguards. In the worst case, a compromised control system can issue any unsafe command that the compromised computer's *hardware* is electrically capable of issuing. All software safeties can be compromised. Misoperation of industrial processes is frequently dangerous, and always costly.

These are not theoretical risks. Cyber-attackers have reached into industrial control systems and sabotaged those systems. Industrial processes have been shut down and costly, difficult-to-replace equipment has been damaged. Some examples: The Stuxnet worm physically destroyed roughly 1,000 uranium enrichment centrifuges in 2010 [3], remote attackers caused massive physical damage to a German steel mill [4], [5], and remote attackers interrupted electric power to nearly one quarter million Ukrainians in 2015 [6].

The Ukrainian attack was noteworthy in that not only were there physical effects from the attack, but SCADA system hard drives were erased, as well as firmware in communications devices. The former could be corrected by re-installing operating system software and restoring other hard drive contents from backups, provided the utility had such backups, and that the backups were sufficiently synchronized with each other version-wise. Erasing device firmware meant that the communications devices had to be completely replaced. With the firmware erased, there was no way to restore the devices to a condition where they worked again. In the parlance of cyber security, this is called "bricking" the devices.

The severity of consequences of misoperation depends on the design and circumstances of the physical process. Poorly designed and operated nuclear generators pose greater threats than poorly-designed or operated washing-machine manufacturing plants. Industrial sites near large population centers are generally of greater concern than sites located far from such centers.

Industrial processes are powerful tools. At most industrial sites, whoever controls the computers, controls the tools. The concern is that every tool is also a weapon – the greater the tool, the greater the weapon.

What's Wrong With This Picture?

All manner of well-meaning SCADA security advice has been published in the last 15 years. Almost all of this advice urges us to deploy more and more software protections and software monitoring systems for our SCADA systems [7], [8], [9]. After all, most of the world's cyber-security experts come from IT networks, where countless software systems are linked inextricably to networks, cell phones and the Internet. So of course, these IT experts believe utterly that the software solutions deployed on their most sophisticated IT networks are the right solutions to apply to the simpler-seeming problems of comparatively-smaller control-system networks.

"Yes, yes" say the IT experts, "we do understand that control systems are a little bit different, but *if we could only somehow* treat control systems exactly the same way as we treat IT systems, then we would see control systems compromised no more often than we see IT networks compromised, and all would be well."

Digging just a little deeper, IT experts tell us that cyber security is all about protecting the data [10], [11]. This is not surprising. The model for the first IT networks was the accounting ledger book. The first IT applications were transaction processing systems and relational databases. Ledger books and accounting systems are all about data, and protecting the data. This mindset carries through to today's IT networks where the focus is still data. IT gurus tell us that IT security is all about protecting the confidentiality, integrity and availability of the data. IT experts tell us that SCADA systems are essentially the same and that we must focus on protecting the data there as well. Only, they tell us, on SCADA networks the priorities are inverted. We are told that SCADA people generally care more about the availability and integrity of data, than its confidentiality.

This is of course, nonsense.

Safety and Reliability

At almost all industrial sites, the first priority is not availability, integrity or confidentiality, but safety: do not kill anyone, do not put public safety at risk, and do not cause an environmental disaster. The second priority is always reliability, not of the control system, but of the physical process. Keep clean water in the distribution system, keep gasoline coming out of the refinery, and keep the lights on. A more or less reliable / available

11

control system is a means to the end of having a very reliable physical process – an ultra-reliable control system is irrelevant if the physical process fails regularly.

Physical safety first, then physical reliability are the priorities. Cyber security is essential to safety and reliability. Any misoperation of the computers controlling our physical process risks misoperation of the physical process itself. Any such misoperation is a threat to both safety and reliability.

Confidentiality, integrity and availability of data do not figure in this calculus at all. Why not? The first SCADA networks did not model accounting ledger books, but dials and gauges. Before there were computers, there were important, often-dangerous industrial processes monitored by analog gauges and controlled by physical, analog, dials and switches. This perspective carries through to today's SCADA networks – the activities on such networks are still very much monitoring and control.

"That's right! That's right!" come the faint voices of the IT guys at the back of the room. "Gauges are monitoring – that's data! Dials and switches are controls, and controls are just 'command messages' and so are also data! It's all data! All we have to do is protect the data!"

Well these people do have one thing right – monitoring is data. Generally speaking, people at industrial sites care very little about who is looking at their gauges or from how far away. Monitoring does not cause disasters.

Control system people however, generally *care enormously* about who is turning the dials and throwing the switches, and care even more that the physical equipment is thus operated safely and reliably. At industrial sites, the first priority for cyber protection of SCADA systems is always preventing unauthorized control. Control "data" is vastly more important than monitoring "data." Calling monitoring and control both "data" blinds us to this essential difference.

Putting IT-class protections in place for monitoring data makes sense. The business and societal consequences of an attacker stealing monitoring data are similar to the consequences of an attacker stealing other kinds of business data. Putting IT-class protections in place for controls is woefully inadequate. At most industrial sites, the consequences of compromised controls are completely unacceptable.

In short, this is the essence of today's SCADA security problem: the data-centric, IT-class protections that so many experts recommend are inadequate to SCADA security needs.

Summary

SCADA systems are powerful tools, and every tool is a weapon, hence the concern about SCADA security.

The first three laws of SCADA security capture essential truths:

1) Nothing is secure
2) All software can be hacked
3) Every piece of information can be an attack

IT experts tell us that if we could only find some way to apply standard IT security technologies to SCADA systems, then all would be well.

They are wrong.

How wrong they are, and why, will become clear in subsequent chapters. For now, consider that the standard advice of IT experts is to "protect the data." Standard IT security advice to "assure the availability and integrity of monitoring and control data" ignores SCADA security priorities and confuses SCADA security programs.

SCADA security priorities are and will always be "don't kill anyone" and "keep the lights on." Cyber security is essential to safety and reliability, but it is safety and reliability that are the priorities.

Recommended Reading

Protecting Industrial Control Systems From Electronic Threats, 2010, by Joe Weiss

SCADA Security

*"Attack is the secret of defense;
defense is the planning of an attack."*

-- Sun Tzu, The Art of War, 5th century BCE

Chapter 3 – Cyber Attacks

If IT-class protections are inadequate, then how should we be protecting SCADA systems? To address this question, we must first understand cyber attacks. Too many SCADA security practitioners do not study modern attack techniques, and so produce singularly vulnerable "secure" SCADA systems.

Instead of attacks, too many of today's SCADA security and IT security practitioners spend far too much time thinking about vulnerabilities. Classic risk assessment calculations maintain that risk is a function of threats, vulnerabilities, exploits and consequences. Many practitioners therefore conclude that their job is to eliminate vulnerabilities. They reason that if we could only, somehow, eliminate all vulnerabilities, then our systems would be *invulnerable*. This chain of reasoning quickly devolves into a preoccupation with known vulnerabilities and security update programs.

This is of course, nonsense.

The first law of cyber security states that nothing is ever secure. For example, security updates repair only known product vulnerabilities, leaving countless unknowns waiting to be discovered and exploited. More generally, SCADA systems as a whole may have vulnerabilities that stem from how the systems are organized and configured, independent of any security defects in product code.

These systems vulnerabilities are at the heart of many kinds of modern attacks. Frankly, our attackers are lazy – they prefer to use permissions we have configured into our SCADA networks rather than software vulnerabilities, because exploiting permissions is less work. It takes considerable time and talent to analyze software applications to find undiscovered software vulnerabilities. It takes even more work to write the code needed to exploit those newly-discovered vulnerabilities.

The standard permissions-based attack described in the section on intelligence agencies below easily defeats security updates, antivirus

15

systems, intrusion detection systems, gazillion-bit-encrypted VPNs[3], remote access jump hosts, firewalls and other IT-class protections routinely installed on SCADA systems. To anyone focused on vulnerabilities rather than attack techniques, this targeted, remote-control, permissions-based type of attack comes as a horrible surprise.

In this chapter, we look at who is attacking us and what their preferred attack patterns look like. The chapter is summarized in Table (1).

	Threat	Resources	Attacks	E.g.
High	Nation States - Military Grade	Nearly unlimited	Autonomous Targeted Malware	Stuxnet
	Intelligence Agencies	Professional	Remote Control Exploit New Vulns	Black Energy
Potential Impact	Hacktivists	Skilled Amateur	Remote Control Exploit Permissions	Ukraine
	SCADA Insiders	Amateur	Exploit Permissions	Maroochy
	Organized Crime	Professional	Indiscriminate Malware, Exploit Known Vulns	Zeus
Low	Corporate Insiders	Amateur	Exploit Permissions	Fraud

Table (1) Threat spectrum

Corporate Insiders

Corporate insiders are people who have access to IT networks, and who are to some degree trusted by the organization. These may be employees,

---

[3] The mathematical strength of cryptosystems increases with the length of the cryptographic key, generally measured in bits. "Gazillion" is formally defined as "any unreasonably large number."

contractors, business partners or even third-party vendors. Insiders generally have some sort of accounts, passwords and other credentials that let them legitimately use equipment and applications on the IT network. These trusted insiders tend to be well-positioned to gain access to additional accounts, passwords and other credentials through social engineering. Social engineering can encompass many activities, for instance, learning other people's passwords by turning their keyboards over and reading the sticky notes on the bottom, impersonating authorized users to distant administrators and asking for password changes, or watching people type as they enter their "strong" passwords.

Corporate insiders though, tend to know little about security and less about industrial control systems. The most common targets of insider attacks are IT systems, yielding either leaked information or financial fraud. Insiders in many organizations have logged into accounting systems, created fictitious vendors, faked invoices and issued payments to themselves either directly or indirectly. Insiders may have the means to steal control-system passwords and log into SCADA systems, but generally lack the skills to do much damage there.

An exception to this rule is corporate IT personnel. For example, well-meaning IT personnel have been known to use administrative privileges on SCADA systems to log in and tell all of the equipment on the SCADA network to reboot. Before coming back online, these administrators apply all outstanding security updates for all software on the machines, carry out full backups of all hard drives to the corporate backup system, and carry out a full antivirus scan. This of course cripples the control system for hours. The plant operator, seeing that she no longer has any way to determine if the physical process is running correctly or safely, has no choice but to lift the cage on the "big red mushroom button," press the button, and trigger a safety shutdown.

This might be funny if it did not cost so very much.

Organized Crime

Organized crime is responsible for the vast majority of email spam and common malware, such as viruses, worms, Trojans, botnets and ransomware. Criminal organizations pay professional malware developers to create these attack tools, and evolve these tools constantly to stay ahead of the professional anti-malware developers producing antivirus, intrusion detection and other anti-malware tools. This is a constant game of cat-and-mouse.

Organized crime has the money and talent to apply to the task of producing malware that spreads indiscriminately and infects or compromises as many machines as possible. This malware generally spreads by deceiving victims into deliberately installing it, or by exploiting known vulnerabilities on machines that have not yet applied security updates. These criminal groups typically extract an average of a few dollars value from each compromised machine. This value may take the form of stolen credit card numbers, bank account credentials, or the use of compromised computers to issue countless millions of spam messages.

The most common impact of such infection is nothing at all – the SCADA system continues unimpeded. Common malware has been known to cause enough symptoms on SCADA systems to trigger shutdowns, but such cases are rare. For example, anecdotal reports from security assessment consultants suggest that a large minority of SCADA systems are still infected with the decade-old Conficker worm, with no apparent ill-effects.

There is a cost to all infections by common malware though: when such infections are discovered, SCADA administrators generally feel obliged to do the work to "clean out" the system. Removing all traces of malware addresses the risk that the malware *may* someday impair important processing. This cleaning can be costly. Removing the most persistent malware often requires the assistance of external, third-party experts.

An exception to this "low impact" rule of thumb is ransomware. Ransomware is malware that encrypts files and demands payment to restore the files. It is easy to imagine how encrypting files on SCADA computers could render important files unusable. This could impair the system enough to affect the operator's confidence levels, thus bringing about a safety shutdown. As ransomware becomes more pervasive, this class of common malware on SCADA networks will become a greater threat to the physical reliability of industrial systems than was the case in the past.

SCADA Insiders

Like IT insiders, SCADA insiders are people with access to SCADA networks and systems who are to some degree trusted by the organization.

Again, they may be employees, contractors or third-party vendors. SCADA insiders generally have some access to accounts, passwords and other credentials that let them use equipment and applications on the SCADA network. As with IT insiders, SCADA insiders tend to be well-positioned to use social engineering attacks to gain additional privileges.

While these insiders often know little about cyber security, they are familiar with industrial systems to a greater or lesser extent. This means that malicious insiders are generally able to manipulate the SCADA systems they log into, and affect physical/industrial operations.

The most common motivation for such insider attacks is revenge for some real or imagined slight.

Hacktivists

Hacktivists are individuals or groups with "an axe to grind" who carry out cyber attacks. Hacktivists often have some degree of security knowledge, and can occasionally be highly skilled – they do after all spend much of their spare time hacking into other people's computers and networks. Hacktivists are amateurs though, in the sense that they generally do not profit personally from breaking into things. This means hacktivists generally cannot afford to purchase the most sophisticated attack tools, and cannot afford to spend the enormous amounts of time and effort needed to write their own world-class hacking tools. This means that hacktivists generally rely on faulty permissions for their attacks, and use open source or other freely-available attack tools.

For example, the December 2015 attack that turned off power to over 200,000 people in Ukraine used typical hacktivist-class attack techniques. Note that this attack was not necessarily carried out by hacktivists – experts argue that the degree of coordination among many attackers in a far-flung attack pattern suggests that professionals were involved.

Published reports however, indicate that no matter who the attackers were, it was only hacktivist-class attack techniques and tools that were used:

- A spear-phishing campaign against employees of electric distribution systems in Ukraine yielded remote access credentials for at least three distribution companies.

- The attackers used these stolen credentials to log in to their targets' networks, look around, and steal additional credentials.
- The attackers used their access to compromise their targets' Windows domain controllers and create new accounts and passwords for themselves, with all the privileges they needed to continue their attacks.
- They then logged into SCADA computers over a period of months, studying how these systems worked. They presumably also used Internet-based and other learning resources to understand how these SCADA systems were designed and configured.
- On the day of the attack, they logged in to at least three distribution companies – published reports include only lower bounds on how many companies were targeted and how many people were affected. On two systems, they activated features of the SCADA software that disabled the operators' mice and keyboards and gave the attackers control of the SCADA HMI. On the third distribution system, the attackers had acquired a copy of the SCADA HMI software on their own computers. To attack this third system, the attackers used a VPN to connect their copy of the SCADA HMI to the distribution system's SCADA infrastructure.
- Over a period of about 30 minutes, the attackers used the HMI software to navigate to screens for at least 30 substations and turn off power flows through those substations. They also logged into the substation control computers and erased the hard drives on those computers so that the computers could not be used to turn on power flows again remotely.

At least 200,000 people were affected for up to several hours. Concurrent with this attack, the attackers flooded the distribution companies' customer support lines with faked phone calls. This way the targets' customers were not able to report that they had no power, which served to increase the duration of the power outage.

This class of attack is known as a "targeted, persistent attack" (TPA) [12]. TPAs differ from more-widely-known, organized-crime attacks in two ways:

1) The attack was most likely motivated by the Ukrainian / Russian conflict, and so had a specific target: distribution companies serving Ukrainian consumers. Even if the attackers had found a dozen less-well-defended targets in neighboring countries, it seems unlikely that they would have been distracted by those targets. The common wisdom of needing only to be protected better than our neighbors does not apply to targeted attacks.

2) This attack used interactive remote control – attackers were sitting at keyboards and giving commands to compromised systems for months before the 30-minute attack on substations, and for the entire duration of the 30-minute substation attack. Common malware spreads indiscriminately, and automatically. Remote-control attacks rely on people "sipping coffee on the other side of the planet" while manually driving the attack, minute by minute.

Note that organized crime has been known to use targeted techniques as well. Ransomware groups have started to seed modified ransomware into networks, to extort larger sums of money for decrypting an entire targeted network than could have been extorted for individual machines [13], [14].

Intelligence Agencies

State-sponsored national and regional intelligence agencies are disciplined groups of attackers using both targeted remote control techniques and when necessary, sophisticated low-volume malware. Different levels of government in China are accused of having pioneered this method of cyber espionage, and many other nations today are accused of using these same techniques. At present, these attacks are used routinely to steal information about dissidents, governments, competing corporations, product designs, source code, and even designs for weapons and industrial sites [15], [16].

Many governments and authorities have expressed concern that these same attack techniques could be used to carry out sabotage rather than espionage. Some governments have declared that sabotage of critical national infrastructures will be regarded as an act of war [17]. This sounds impressive, but reliable attribution of this class of attack to specific state or private actors can be difficult or impossible. For example, the "Shamoon" malware erased the hard drives of 30,000 IT computers at Saudi Aramco, crippling business functions [18]. In spite of claims by what appears to be an Iranian hacktivist group, and widespread speculation that the group acted with the support of Iran's government [19], no reliable attribution was ever published, nor were military or other retaliatory steps taken against any nation.

Worse, these intelligence-agency-grade attack techniques are not limited to use by nation-states. Any organization with a budget to develop custom malware can develop the ability to use these techniques. Many experts are concerned that organized crime will start using this class of attack to sabotage industrial sites in order to extort money from those sites, manipulate stock markets or otherwise derive significant profits from cyber-sabotage attacks.

A typical attack of this type has many steps:

1) The attackers scour social networking sites for personal information and use spear-phishing techniques to deceive an individual in a targeted organization into clicking on an attachment or downloading a file, to activate a malware payload.

2) Antivirus (AV) sensors in the targeted organization are blind to the attack, because the payload has been used sparingly. AV sensors are designed to defeat high-volume, organized-crime malware. New AV signatures are created when an AV vendor detects many thousands of copies of a new variant of malware on the vendor's Internet honeypot machines. Intelligence-agency-class malware is typically deployed to a few hundred victims' sites at most. The malware does not spread automatically, and so never reaches AV-vendor honeypots on the Internet. This means no AV vendor produces AV signatures for the malware.

3) The malware payload "phones home." connecting to and reporting to an Internet command and control (C&C) center. Professional operators use the C&C to connect to the malware and operate it remotely. This class of malware often has features built into it that are similar to popular "secure shell" and "remote desktop" remote access tools. The malware allows remote operators to issue commands to compromised machines, see the results of those commands, and even take over the screen, keyboard and mouse.

4) The malware's operators use compromised computers to look around the compromised network very quietly, spread the malware to other machines where the compromised account might

have permissions to create and run executable files, and most importantly, steal account names and passwords.

5) When the attackers steal Windows domain administrator credentials, they often create new administrator and VPN accounts for themselves, so that they no longer need to use their special malware to continue the attack. They also use these credentials to pivot deeper, through intervening firewalls and other layers of protection, into more-protected networks such as SCADA networks.

6) When they reach their goals, they are in a position to start stealing large volumes of information, modifying information or misoperating industrial systems.

For high-value targets, the attackers may seed several kinds of malware in the target organizations, each reporting to a different control center. The least-valuable, least-sophisticated malware is used first. This may be a standard attack tool circulating free on the Internet. If that tool is detected and erased, the attackers can fall back to more-sophisticated tools, such as those available on black markets. If these tools are detected and cleaned out of the target system, they may revert to their own, custom-written, highly-stealthed tools to re-establish their presence on the compromised network at some later time, when the site's investigation and clean-up of the less-valuable tools is complete.

This class of attack has been extremely effective and is very hard to detect. Authorities and researchers investigating some C&C centers often find evidence that large numbers of organizations have been compromised. When these authorities reach out to these targeted organizations, the vast majority report that they had no idea they had been compromised.

For example, in the Ukrainian attack, post-incident investigators found BlackEnergy malware on SCADA computers. BlackEnergy is a sophisticated malware tool with many features, including full remote control of compromised computers. The investigators reported that while they believed the BlackEnergy malware had enough features to carry out the attack on the power system, there was no evidence the malware was in fact part of the attack, or that the malware was even deployed by the same attack group.

That said, intelligence-agency-class attacks often use the simplest attack methods available. Such an adversary might use a hacktivist-class remote access attack, with more sophisticated tools such as the BlackEnergy malware kept in reserve until they might become necessary.

Military-Grade

Nothing is secure. Military-grade attacks prove this point. Military-grade attacks not only have access to all of the attack techniques used by all of the other classes of attackers, they have enormous financial and technical resources, as well as physical attack techniques to fall back on. Military-grade attacks can physically break into targets to steal their private encryption keys and other credentials. They can intercept equipment and software on the way to customers, and insert custom hardware and malware into those shipments. Military-grade attackers can pay large sums of money for newly-discovered "zero-day" vulnerabilities in applications and cyber-security products and defenses, and can pay more money to produce custom malware to exploit and weaponize those vulnerabilities. These attackers can deceive, buy, blackmail, or otherwise coerce cooperation from trusted insiders at a target site.

If an attacker has the means to bribe or coerce insiders into revealing all of the details of how an industrial system is designed, and how that industrial system is protected, and that attacker has the means to find vulnerabilities in and defeat any cyber security protections, then such an attacker's target does not have a true cyber-security problem. There is no cyber-security technology the site can deploy that will defeat this grade of attacker reliably.[4] Instead, the industrial site has a classic cold-war-style cyber-espionage problem, and really needs to escalate that problem to its own national intelligence agencies.

Stuxnet is widely regarded as the best-documented example of a military-grade attack. In this example, the attackers appear to have deceived insiders, and may not have needed to coerce or bribe them. The attackers though, certainly appear to have had the means to produce a very

---

[4] We offer a proof by example: imagine an organization whose CEO is concerned that her organization is the target of a cyber assault. In fact, every employee and vendor in the organization has been bought or coerced by a foreign power. What cyber-security technology can the CEO order put in place that will defend against this military-grade assault?

expensive, very powerful, very complex piece of autonomous attack malware. Chapter 7 holds a more-detailed discussion of Stuxnet.

Transmitting Attacks

Cyber attacks are information, and are embedded in information. Every piece of information can be an attack, even a single one/zero bit, and even information transmitted using analog signaling. What does this mean?

Pretty much everyone knows that sophisticated attack code can be embedded in complex files, such as PDF files. Any communications mechanism that transmits files, including people carrying such files on removable media or cell phones in so-called "sneakernet" communications, can transmit attack code. Most people know that any continuous stream of complex messages can encode attacks as well, such as message streams arriving across the Internet. Most of us also know that a compromised machine can be used to pivot attacks to heavily-protected targets through one or several more-easily-accessible targets.

Many people though, even security experts who should know better, regard the simplest and most primitive analog signaling systems as "secure" in the sense that they believe that attacks cannot be communicated through such mechanisms. For example, an electric signal on a network cable can indicate whether a connected device is turned on or turned off, even if no messages are exchanged on the wire. Experts sometimes recommend that this sort of primitive signaling be used when a very small number of simple values must be communicated from external systems into a SCADA system. These experts may regard such signaling mechanisms as too primitive to communicate an attack, even though they do communicate very small amounts of information.

In practice, such signals do communicate information, and so even these most primitive signals can constitute an attack, in two different ways:

- When the signal is used as a control signal, indicating that, for example, a motor should be turned on or off, or a valve should be opened or closed, the signal may be deliberately incorrect. In this way, a compromised source for the signal may misoperate an industrial process or device.
- More subtly, if malware has somehow been planted in the SCADA system, any signal entering the system can be used to trigger the

operation of the malware. The on/off signal may itself serve to activate and de-activate the malware, or the timing of the signal may serve that function, or some other characteristic of the signal.

Again, any information at all, however simple-seeming or benign-seeming, can be an attack. If we want to understand how we can be attacked, we must study how information moves into our SCADA systems from potentially-compromised and potentially-malicious sources.

Summary

SCADA security practitioners must focus on attacks, not vulnerabilities. Hacktivist-class attacks operate by remote control, and routinely defeat security systems with permissions rather than software vulnerabilities. Intelligence agencies also attack by remote control, and can do so with hacktivist-class techniques, or with remote-control malware.

These modern, remote-control attacks routinely defeat IT-centric security measures such as two-factor authentication, passwords, firewalls, antivirus systems and security-update programs. At the high end of our threat spectrum, we face nearly-unlimited attack capabilities. Nothing is secure.

The movement of information is essential in carrying out attacks. Attacks are information, even if that information is only a password and malicious intent in the head of an insider. Every bit of information can be an attack, including every message, and every storage device.

Do not despair though. With this understanding of attacks, we consider costly, ineffective, IT-class defenses in Chapter 4, and then look at much more effective SCADA-focused defenses in Chapter 5.

Recommended Reading

Mandiant APT1 – Exposing One of China's Cyber Espionage Units, 2013, by Mandiant

Hacking Exposed Industrial Control Systems: ICS and SCADA Security Secrets & Solutions, 2016, by Clint Bodungen, Bryan Singer, Aaron Shbeeb, Kyle Wilhoit, and Stephen Hilt

"If I had a hammer,
I'd hammer in the morning.
I'd hammer in the evening..."
-- *Pete Seeger & Lee Hays, 1949*

Chapter 4 – Failure of Defense In Depth

In response to the attacks described in Chapter 3, and many other kinds of attacks, the IT approach to cyber security has been held up as the "gold standard" for SCADA security, pretty much ever since SCADA security started. SCADA security emerged as a discipline only after the World Trade Center attack in 2001, and naturally took inspiration from what was then the more mature IT security field. This tendency to take inspiration from IT security was reinforced by the IT software and hardware products that had become nearly ubiquitous in control systems by the early 2000s.

What most people recognized almost immediately was that some IT techniques were a poor fit for the needs of SCADA systems, which led to a doctrine of "compensating measures" and "defense in depth." IT reasoning here postulates that if we cannot solve some of the security problems directly, we need to put compensating measures in place. A comprehensive system of such measures was seen as a "defense in depth" posture, where "layers of security" would save us from the innate limitations of any single defensive measure.

Defense in depth has failed. Modern attacks routinely compromise both IT and SCADA networks protected by IT-style defense-in-depth systems. SCADA security standards, regulations and advice are evolving beyond IT defense-in-depth, but only slowly. In spite of its clear deficiencies, many experts, and especially IT experts, still maintain that IT-style defense-in-depth is the right approach for SCADA security. It is after all, the "hammer" they know.

To understand why defense in depth has failed, we examine the IT-style approach to SCADA security in this chapter. The approach is summarized in Table (2). In the table, the line demarking the boundary between threats we are reasonably confident of defeating reliably, and threats we are not confident of defeating reliably, is labelled as the design-basis threat. Design-basis threat is a concept from physical security. A design-basis threat document describes the most capable adversary a site

27

is required to defeat with a high degree of confidence. At many sites, the document is confidential or classified.

	Threat	Defense	Cost	Effect
Design-Basis Threat	Nation-State Military	Escalate to national agencies	n/a	
	Intelligence Agencies	IDS / Exfiltration prevention	$$$$	Poor
	Hacktivists	Intrusion detection systems	$$$$	Fair
	SCADA Insiders	Physical security, detailed auditing	$$	Good
	Organized Crime	Encryption, AV, security updates	$$$	Good
	Corporate Insiders	Firewalls, role-based permissions	$	Fair

Table (2): IT-centric Defense In Depth

Corporate Insiders

IT-style defense in depth starts with the simplest threat – corporate insiders. The receptionist's computer in an office on another continent should not be able to send messages that confuse a control system. And so, the first defense most sites deploy is a firewall.

What is a firewall exactly? A firewall is a router with a filter.

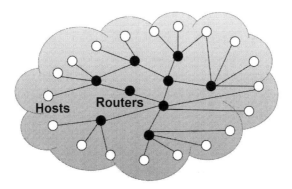

Figure (1): A simple model of the Internet

What is a router? Well, one simple way to think of the Internet is as illustrated in Figure (1). The Internet is a great many computers, routers, and the connections – wired, wireless or fibre-optic – between those computers and routers. The computers create and consume Internet Protocol (IP) messages. That is, the computers are the sources and destinations of IP messages. Routers are special-purpose devices running software that determines the paths to use through the twisty maze of connections to deliver IP messages from the computers producing the messages to the computers that are the destinations of those messages. Routers receive messages all day long, determine what path each message should use to arrive to its destination, and then forward each message to the connection that delivers the message to the next router in the message's path.

A firewall's filter is also software. The filter software examines each message and asks, "Is this message allowed?" If the message matches a filter rule, and does not seem to be an attack message, the filter tells the router part of the firewall "looks OK, send it on" and the router forwards the message. The problem of course, is that no filter is or ever can be perfect. When the filter fails to identify an attack, the firewall forwards attack messages, generally right into the SCADA network the firewall is supposed to be protecting. In practice, there are many ways to defeat firewalls [20].

Defense in depth, therefore, teaches us to deploy several layers of firewalls between our SCADA systems and the Internet, each from a different vendor, and to use different kinds of communications across each layer. The reasoning here is that when vulnerabilities are found in firewalls, communications protocols, and other systems, this design reduces the likelihood that a single vulnerability will provide an attacker with a pivoting path through the multiple layers of defenses.

To reach a SCADA system through a system of networks designed with defense-in-depth in mind, a corporate insider would need to find a way to pivot through one firewall and computer system after another. If we assume that the corporate insiders we are protecting against are technically unsophisticated, such a design may be enough to slow them down, or stop them entirely. More sophisticated attackers are slowed very little by only layers of firewalls, as we will see shortly.

Very often, the next step in a new security program is accounts, permissions, and passwords. To keep nosy, curious or malicious corporate insiders out of the SCADA systems accessible through each layer of firewall, we configure those SCADA systems and sometimes the firewalls themselves with accounts, passwords, and sometimes a two-factor password-generation device, or a finger-print swipe. Oh yes – and do not forget password complexity. Passwords do no good if they are weak and everyone can guess them, so we had better give those accounts long, complex, hard-to-remember passwords and require our users to change those passwords frequently. This makes it harder to guess passwords and to steal them by looking over somebody's shoulder.

The obvious problem here is that there are hundreds of computers in a typical SCADA system, and there is no human way to remember hundreds of hard-to-remember passwords, much less change them every few weeks. So IT security teaches us to purchase, deploy, configure and manage single-sign-on systems, such as Windows Active Directory servers. This way each of our people needs to remember only one hard-to-remember password, and needs to change that one password on only one system every 90 days or so. All of the SCADA systems ask the Active Directory authentication server to do all the password checking for the SCADA network.

Not only does this simplify password management for our people, IT security teaches us that this helps us manage our workforce very closely. For example, if one of our users leaves the business, or transfers to a different division, we can revoke all of that user's permissions on all machines, with a single mouse-click. Different IT-centric security standards in fact demand that when someone leaves unexpectedly, that this person's permissions be revoked in as little as one to twenty-four hours, depending on the standard, the sensitivity of the installation and the circumstances of the person leaving. Such aggressive permissions management is difficult without some kind of central password manager.

The problem here is that IT-centric security and standards teach us to ignore the new risk we have just introduced. The new risk is that the new central password management system also constitutes a new single point of compromise for all of our SCADA systems. If an attacker somehow persuades the central password-management system to create a new administrator account with universal privileges, then that attacker can use the new account to misoperate any part of any SCADA system exposed through a firewall. They can further use footholds reachable through a firewall to pivot attacks through firewalls deeper into SCADA systems, to reach even safety and equipment-protection systems with no apparent connectivity to external networks such as the Internet.

IT teaches us that the benefit of central password administration is greater than the risk of a single point of compromise. This is foolish. Our enemies rejoice when they find such single points of compromise, and take advantage of them routinely.

It gets worse. If there is a safety emergency, such as a fire in the facility, and the plant operator hears the alarm going, sees the room filling with smoke and knows she has to get out of the room quickly if she is ever to see her children again, will she remember the password for the emergency systems? In an emergency, people are under enormous stress. Scientists have studied this kind of stress at length. Bluntly, almost all of us become markedly stupider when we are under this kind of stress.

Those of us who have trouble remembering our passwords on a good day are doomed if we need to remember a password to save our lives. Thus, if we are to deploy accounts and passwords on our SCADA systems, we need to pay our engineers to review or repeat some or all of their safety studies. We need to ensure that password protections are not putting people's lives at risk, or putting the reliability of the physical process at risk. Security after all, is supposed to be about enhancing safety and reliability, not impairing them.

None of these safety problems is news to the SCADA security world. The IT-based defense-in-depth advice out there all talks about these problems and advises us to "bite the bullet" and put passwords and permissions everywhere we possibly can. This advice teaches us to redo all of our safety analyses and emergency planning if necessary, and to disable passwords only for those systems that absolutely cannot tolerate passwords. IT security then advises that when the lack of passwords on some of our SCADA computers makes our systems unacceptably insecure, we must deploy additional, costly, compensating measures and layers of defenses.

Organized Crime

Next, IT-style defense in depth recommends deploying antivirus systems and security updates or "patches" in the language of SCADA systems. The antivirus systems should catch the majority of high-volume malware that sneaks in through the firewall and on USB drives, and the security updates should block the rest. Almost all of the high-volume malware in the world exploits known vulnerabilities, and software updates eliminate such vulnerabilities.

Here the problems with the IT-centric approach start in earnest. We all know how hard it is to get any work done on a computer that is doing a full antivirus scan, even a brand new computer with the newest, ultra-modern, antivirus system on it. This is why the AV system schedules scans infrequently, and most often in the dead of night. These systems also generally open up a handy window for us on the screen when a scan is in progress, so we can suspend the scan if we happen to be awake, trying to work.

Every AV system really does need to do a full scan from time to time, in case there is something in the filesystem the AV system's real-time monitoring has missed. If we disable full scans, we seriously limit the usefulness of the AV system. The problem with SCADA systems is scheduling the scan. When is it that we can afford to have any part of the SCADA system slow down so badly that the system operator is no longer able to effectively monitor or control our important, complex, and sometimes dangerous physical processes? With most plants, we have plant operators sitting in front of the SCADA system 24x7, for years at a time, because we are aiming for zero downtime. Antivirus scanning is a real problem on our most important SCADA computers.

Security updates are worse. Ask any plant engineer what it takes to bring a plant up to full capacity after a complete refit. Take a refinery for example. A typical refinery shuts down completely every few years for a full inspection, repair, and upgrade. Worn components are repaired or replaced. The SCADA group uses the opportunity to replace almost all of the computer components and upgrade software systems as much as possible, system-wide, to reflect the most recent stable versions, with the very latest security updates. Many teams, for many years, tend to plan for and prepare for such downtime opportunities. When the plant starts up again it is essentially "as good as new" and is ready to run for another half decade.

The problem is this. Such a refit entails a great deal of change. Change is the enemy of safety and reliability. When we start up again after touching and possibly changing everything, how do we know that the system is acceptably safe? At most sites the answer is, "We don't."

Safety and reliability engineering plays a huge role in the planning and execution of such refits, but safety and reliability are continuous, just like security. Nothing can ever be "safe," only "safe enough with respect to defined risks." In spite of the enormous amount of planning, engineering and testing going into a project such as this one, there is always the risk of a miscalculation or mistake. This makes the start-up process painstaking. All vacation is cancelled, all weekends are cancelled and "all hands are on deck." Every one of the system's contractors and systems integrators are present as well. Everyone starts working 12 hour days as the plant is started and brought to 5% of capacity.

The entire team, engineers, technicians and all, walks around looking at almost everything, listening to things, touching, even smelling things. The computer people are logged in looking at log files, debugging traces, memory usage and network messages. We find problems, yes, and fix them. After a number of days, the plant is brought up to 25% of capacity, and the process continues. More problems are found, and fixed. 50%. 75%. After about three weeks of this, the plant is at 100% of capacity. People are getting a little squirrely by this time, but we keep at it, looking, listening, and checking. Eventually, we stop finding serious new problems. We have fixed the most important problems. We have logged, analyzed, planned & scheduled fixes for the less important problems.

After three-ish weeks, the team starts standing down. We cut back to regular-length shifts. We start letting people taking a day off to see their children again. The contractors start going home. After a full month, the plant is working at 100% of capacity and everything is back to normal.

The next day Microsoft issues 73 security updates to 73 parts of the Windows operating system running on the computers at the plant. Microsoft gives very little detail as to how much code has changed, or how the code has changed. The SCADA vendor provides no guidance at all as to whether it is "safe" to deploy the changed code at this particular plant, taking into consideration the specific configuration of computers on this plant's SCADA networks. Neither does the operating system or SCADA vendor explain how likely it is that any of the changes will trigger an unexpected shutdown of important parts of the SCADA system.

Are we going to deploy those security updates on all of the SCADA computers the day after Microsoft issues them, to stay "secure?" If we do, how do we know the changed systems are still sufficiently safe and reliable? Shall we apply the updates, call everyone back and start at 5% again? If not, how much testing should we repeat to ensure the plant is still acceptably safe?

Almost nobody deploys security updates on SCADA systems without extensive, costly testing. There is simply no way to predict the consequences of changed code without seeing the source code, and frankly, we probably would not understand most of the source code if we did see it. In truth, in many software systems, the code's own maintainers barely understand how the code works.

Some SCADA sites spend large sums of money to build more or less complete copies of their SCADA systems on test beds, complete with physical process simulators, so they can test the updates before deploying them. The testing process is exhaustive, and costly. Months after the updates are available, we start deploying them to *some* of the SCADA computers – the least important and most expendable ones. We then watch those computers for a period of time to see how they perform. Then we deploy to more-important computers and watch them, and so on. Other sites say "nuts to that" and simply do not patch until the next major refit. The IT approach to security updates amounts to "constant, aggressive change to 'stay ahead of the bad guys,'" but change is the enemy of safety and of reliability. "Engineering change control" is how we must manage SCADA networks, not "constant aggressive change."

None of this is news. The IT-based defense-in-depth advice out there all talks about this problem and advises us to evaluate our risks carefully, and test our security updates "adequately" before we deploy those updates. The advice tells us to apply security updates as frequently as we can, on only those systems where we can, given the physical, safety and reliability constraints under which we work. Such advice also reminds us that the vulnerabilities in our SCADA systems do not go away simply because we are unable to apply antivirus systems or security updates to our most important computers. This advice reminds us that if we cannot eliminate software and systems vulnerabilities with security updates, we must deploy some other kind of compensating measure or measures to address those vulnerabilities.

SCADA Insiders

Control system insiders are, again, people with legitimate physical and logical access to control system equipment. These people pose a unique threat. On the one hand, they have logical access and often physical access to control system equipment, and so are uniquely well-equipped to damage that equipment if they choose to do so. On the other hand, if they act to damage equipment or impair safety, it is their own health and well-being they may put at risk.

Classic cyber security suggests that the best way to address this risk is with a combination of measures.

- Deploy physical access controls, to ensure that only authorized insiders have physical access to industrial equipment and control system equipment,
- Pay and treat our people well, and fairly, and so dramatically reduce the likelihood that a SCADA insider will develop malicious intent,
- Carry out personnel background checks and monitoring, to identify individuals who might be at higher-than-usual risk of becoming disgruntled or coerced,
- Set up video monitoring to provide some chance of catching physical sabotage in the act, but more to provide evidence for post-attack investigations, and

35

- Set up detailed cyber auditing and monitoring, again primarily to provide evidence for post-attack investigations.

The detailed physical and cyber monitoring serve to deter insider attacks, by making successful prosecution of offending insiders very likely. To be effective as a deterrent though, such monitoring should be visible, but this must be balanced against giving the impression to SCADA insiders that they are not trusted.

In practice, SCADA insiders are the most trusted individuals in the business when it comes to the industrial equipment they operate. In practice, these detailed monitoring records can and should be used routinely to investigate safety incidents and plant shutdowns. The recordings are therefore positioned as tools to improve worker safety and uptime. Video monitoring and other audit records can be very visible in their role as tools to improve safety and reliability, and this visibility helps to deter insider attacks.

Hacktivists

By this time in our IT-style defense-in-depth design, we have built up a lot of residual risk and have only talked about compensating measures, not implemented any. At this point in the design, and to address hacktivist threats as well, IT-style defense-in-depth brings out the "big guns:" intrusion detection systems (IDSs). Intrusion detection systems monitor logs, network activity, computer/host activity, physical access systems and other systems, looking for suspicious activity. IDSs are positioned by IT gurus, and of course by everyone selling intrusion detection systems, as the pinnacle of any defense-in-depth program. Given the residual risks in our defensive systems, and given the capabilities of our enemies, our IT gurus submit that compromise of our most important networks is inevitable.

IT gurus tell us that the best hope we have of addressing this inevitable compromise is to assume that our systems have been compromised and actively go out looking for the compromised equipment. When we find compromised equipment, we had better have practiced incident response teams available to isolate, clean out, and restore the affected systems from backups. In addition, IT experts tell us we should really have an information sharing system in place as well, so that we can learn from other sites who have discovered compromised equipment, and so we can share with others what we have learned from compromised equipment we find at our sites.

Sounds convincing, doesn't it?

There are serious problems with this approach. We begin with the last paragraph above. IDSs are a detective measure, not a preventive one – IDSs do not prevent compromise. A recent survey of North American energy sector executives showed that the average executive was convinced that their SCADA systems' intrusion detection systems would detect any intrusion within 24 hours of the intrusion [21]. Other studies though, show that the *average* intrusion takes six months to detect and remediate [22].

One of these numbers must be wrong.

In a sense though, it does not matter which number is wrong. Either way, whether it is for 24 hours or 24 months, for all of that time our enemies have remote control of part or all of our SCADA systems. This is an unacceptable risk. After all, we cannot restore tainted water, damaged turbines, or human lives, "from backups."

It gets worse. Not only is the effectiveness of intrusion detection unacceptably limited, to be effective at all intrusion detection must be very costly. This is because no IDS is or ever can be perfect. There is simply no way to distinguish legitimate activity from illegitimate activity reliably. This means that all intrusion detection systems must be tuned, to be more or less sensitive. The more sensitive we make an IDS, the more legitimate activity it diagnoses as potential intrusions. These are called "false alarms" or "false positives." The less sensitive we make an IDS, the more intrusions it misses. These are called "missed attacks" or "false negatives."

To be confident of missing a minimum of real attacks, an IDS must produce many false alarms. The problem is that there is no way to automatically distinguish real attacks from false alarms, and put a green "false alarm" icon over the alarms our security team can safely ignore. To find the real attacks, we need to pay experts to investigate all of the alarms, including countless false alarms. We could of course, reduce the sensitivity of the IDS so that it never produces false alarms. Unfortunately, this generally means the IDS never produces alarms at all, and so would miss all of the real attacks as well.

None of this is news. In spite of these problems, all IT-based defense-in-depth advice positions IDSs, "practiced incident response teams," and "information sharing networks" as the most effective compensating measures in a defense-in-depth program. IT advice pretty much assumes a constant, high rate of false alarms. This is after all how we keep our costly incident response teams well-practiced.

Intelligence Agencies

Thus far, the world's cyber-intelligence agencies appear to have focused more on cyber-espionage than cyber-sabotage. IT-style defense-in-depth advises us to address this threat by deploying "data exfiltration prevention" technologies. This class of technologies covers a wide variety of techniques including detecting the operation of tools that search for and gather data, detecting the transmission of data to external sites, encrypting data so that when it is stolen, it cannot be decrypted and is therefore worthless, and so on.

There are many problems with this approach. The biggest is that we are solving the wrong problem on SCADA networks. Intelligence-agency-class attacks can carry out sabotage as easily as espionage, and what we really want is to protect against sabotage. Next-biggest is that, like intrusion detection systems, most data-exfiltration-prevention technologies are more detective than preventive. These technologies do not prevent compromise and misoperation of our networks and physical infrastructure, they merely alert us when someone is stealing large amounts of our data.

To an extent, this *is* news to IT security people, and to SCADA security people. These modern, powerful, intelligence-agency-class attacks are comparatively new, and are credited with having broken into large numbers of apparently well-defended IT and SCADA networks, world-wide. Thus far, the IT response to this threat to safety and reliability has been muddled. That response is perhaps best summed up as the experts telling us "Err – try harder with your intrusion detection systems on your SCADA networks would you?"

Military-Grade

Nothing is secure. This is something that a lot of people, even experts, forget frequently. A great deal of utter nonsense has been written about how to protect a site against a military-class attack, and a Stuxnet-like attack in particular – see Chapter 7 for details.

For example, some experts are on record saying that nuclear reactor control systems, and even safety networks for those reactors, should be connected all the way out to the Internet behind layers of firewalls, antivirus systems, intrusion detection systems and every other bit of IT security software they can imagine. This is in spite of such designs being effectively illegal in many jurisdictions. In spite of these laws and regulations, we have some IT experts saying, "No! No! Connect it all! It's safer that way!"

Few in any industry have anything good to say about cyber-security regulators. We should all however, thank our law-makers for the nuclear regulators who keep us safe from these well-meaning but hopelessly misguided IT security people [23], [24], [25].

Constant Compromise

The above discussion can be very distressing to anyone who has not seen it before. If IT-class protections are this ineffective, why does anyone use these protections, even on IT networks?

On IT networks, we have no choice. Consider that an IT network in a large organization permits hundreds of thousands or even millions of electronic mail messages to enter the network every day. A little less than 1% of these messages contain attacks of some sort. IT teams deploy technology to screen incoming messages and web pages for phishing attacks or other harmful content, but no screening technology is or can ever be perfect. Even if the screening technology is 99% accurate, which none is, at least tens or hundreds of attack messages are permitted into the IT network every week. At least that many malicious web pages arrive in an IT network every day, as well. Studies have shown that no matter how vigorously an organization trains its people, a large fraction of people in almost all organizations are regularly deceived by phishing attacks [26], [27], [28].

As a result of all this, most large IT networks contain compromised computers, most of the time. This is why we deploy intrusion detection systems on IT networks, to try to find the compromised machines. This is why we have practiced incident response systems and teams. In large networks, those teams are tracking down and cleaning our compromised equipment, pretty much constantly. Constant compromise is the natural state of any IT network that permits this many attacks to enter the network every day.

We might like to stop attacks from entering our IT networks, but we cannot. All information can be an attack, and we have a large, constant flow of complex information into our IT networks in the form of electronic mail, web pages and other content.

The real puzzle here is not why our IT networks are in a state of constant compromise. The real puzzle is why IT security experts routinely recommend these limited-effectiveness, IT-class protections for SCADA systems controlling important, complex, and sometimes dangerous physical processes.

Summary

IT security tools are costly, with serious limitations. Security updates are changes to reliability-critical or safety-critical code, and are very costly to test. The most sensitive intrusion detection systems generate large numbers of false-positive alarms, each of which must be investigated by incident response teams. Worse, intrusion detection systems are detective measures, not preventive measures. An intruder has remote access to our SCADA system for at least as long as it takes to discover and investigate an IDS alarm.

Modern, remote-control attacks routinely exploit single-point-of-compromise domain controllers, pivot through firewalls, and defeat antivirus, security update and intrusion detection systems. IT-class security mechanisms struggle to defeat hacktivist-class and more-capable attacks at all reliably. As a result, IT networks are more or less constantly compromised.

The real puzzle here is why IT security experts continue to recommend these limited, IT-class protections to our SCADA networks.

Recommended Reading

Recommended Practice: Improving Industrial Control Systems Cybersecurity with Defense-In-Depth Strategies, 2009, U.S. Department of Homeland Security

"An ounce of prevention is worth a pound of cure."

-- Benjamin Franklin, 1734

Chapter 5 – Preventing Intrusion

Today's alternative approach to IT-centric SCADA security started seeing widespread discussion in 2009 or so. Instead of focusing on software-based protections with intrusion detection and incident response capabilities, the modern approach focuses on hardware-based capabilities to prevent intrusions and compromise. In SCADA systems, preventing intrusion must always be the first priority and the second priority as well. We cannot after all, restore human lives or damaged equipment "from backups" the way we can with IT systems. However, how are we to prevent attacks, if the attacks, the defenses and the SCADA systems themselves are as complex as they seem thus far in our discussion?

To defend our plants, we simplify. Consider a power plant, or a refinery. The site has a fence around it, and guards with guns at the gates. This is a physical barrier to the movement of people and certain materials into and out of the facility[5]. Inside the fence is a "cyber perimeter" as well – a barrier to the movement of certain kinds of information into and out of the facility.

While the variety of sophisticated cyber attacks on SCADA systems may seem infinite, there is one universal, common characteristic. For a SCADA system to change from an uncompromised to a compromised state, an attack must somehow cross the perimeter of the SCADA system. All cyber attacks are information. Attack information might be a buffer-overflow attack in a message, or a corrupt file on a USB drive carried into the facility, or a password and malicious intent in the brain of an insider who we allow to touch control equipment inside the facility. For an attack to reach a SCADA system, the attack must cross either the physical perimeter or cyber perimeter.

Now, many IT security gurus tell us "the perimeter is dead" and that the only hope for the future of IT security is skillful, practiced, intrusion

---

[5] Yes, drones are a new problem for physical perimeter protection. Anti-drone defenses will emerge as a new market very quickly.

detection and response teams [29]. They point out how in most businesses, enormous amounts of company-confidential information is resident on cell phones, and that increasing use of cloud computing, "bring your own device" computing and other trends are erasing the physical and network perimeters of modern businesses [30].

This may be true of IT network perimeters, but is it true of SCADA network perimeters? "Yes of course" come the faint cries from the IT guys at the back of the room. "The Industrial Internet of Things is coming, haven't you heard?!"

Well, the industrial Internet is coming, but consider the nuclear safety system example once more. Imagine we are building a brand new nuclear power plant, and we just purchased a state of the art Industrial Internet of Things (IIoT) digital safety system. To re-emphasize, this is not a state-of-the-practice system. This is a *state-of-the-art* system, endowed with every bit of software and hardware protection that anyone has ever imagined. Our imaginary system uses trusted platform hardware modules, proven-correct hypervisors, gazillion-bit encryption and every other security mechanism known to humankind. Our IIoT safety system is self-organizing, self-defending and "completely secure."

Is there anyone in the world who would connect this nuclear-reactor safety system directly to the Internet?

Well, there are IT fools who might. Safety engineers will never do so. No matter how much software security is built into a system, there is always the risk of a vulnerability. No safety system needs to receive messages from the other side of the world to operate correctly, and so there is no reason to permit attack packets from all over the planet to test the safety system for vulnerabilities all day long. This is why we always deploy a cyber perimeter around our nuclear, chemical, electrical and other safety systems. For that matter, we always deploy a cyber perimeter around our reliability-critical systems as well. This is in addition to the physical perimeter protecting the general public from the our dangerous physical process, and vice-versa. Perimeters may be dead on IT networks, but they are vital to many kinds of SCADA networks.

Perimeters also provide a way for us to understand attack vectors. Every message inbound through a cyber perimeter can encode an attack, as can every CD or USB drive, every computer, and every piece of physical equipment that we carry in our site with computers embedded in the equipment. This is essential to the SCADA security problem – the flow of information and hardware *into SCADA systems* through cyber and physical perimeters is our only attack vector.

Having thus defined and understood the problem, we can see how to solve it. And yes, appropriate security for an IIoT deployment is somewhat more complex. In Chapter 12 we will apply the solutions below to the IIoT problem.

Top-Down Security

The SCADA approach to security starts with the most sophisticated adversary we need to defeat reliably. We would like to be able to defeat all attacks, but the first law says nothing is secure. There is no security technology that can reliably defeat the essentially unlimited resources of a military-grade adversary, able to buy or blackmail all of our employees, and all of the employees at all of our vendors. So we start one rung down the threat spectrum.

Almost every SCADA system should be able to defeat reliably, essentially all those attacks that are less capable than the most sophisticated military-grade assault.

The most sophisticated attacks mounted by intelligence agencies with supporting professional-grade malware developers, are custom-malware-based, remote-control attacks. Like the attack on the power system in Ukraine, these attacks work across the Internet. Our enemies can be sipping coffee on another continent as they reach through firewalls and defense-in-depth IT-class defenses to sabotage our SCADA systems.

Intelligence Agencies

To address these attacks, we draw our design-basis threat line through our threat spectrum just below unlimited-capability, military-grade attacks, as illustrated in Table (3). We start our defensive posture by deploying unidirectional gateways as the sole connection between the protected SCADA system and any outside network. In short, unidirectional gateways are hardware that can send information out to the world through a cyber perimeter, and are physically unable to send any information at all back into the SCADA system. More specifically, since all attacks are information, the gateways permit monitoring information to leave a SCADA network, without letting any information / attacks back in.

Recall that most SCADA system operators do not care who looks at their gauges, but care enormously who is turning the dials, and whether the dials are turned to a safe, correct setting. Unlike firewalls, unidirectional gateways permit remote monitoring, while reliably defeating remote control. Unidirectional gateways are described in detail in Chapter 6.

	Threat	Defense	Cost	Eff
Design-Basis Threat	Nation-State Military	Escalate to national agencies	n/a	
	Intelligence Agencies	Unidirectional Gateways	$	Good
	Hacktivists	done	n/a	Good
	SCADA Insiders	Physical security / detailed auditing	$$	Good
	Organized Crime	Media / device controls	$	Good
	Corporate Insiders	done	n/a	Good

Table (3) Top-Down Security Posture

Hacktivists

Further down the threat list are hacktivist-class remote-control attacks. These too are reliably defeated by unidirectional gateways. No remote control attacks can enter protected SCADA systems through outbound-oriented unidirectional gateways.

SCADA Insiders

Next on the list are malicious SCADA insiders. The usual measures all apply here, including video & cyber monitoring, physical perimeters, paying our people well, treating them well, as well as secondary measures such as role-based security and passwords.

When we deploy security mechanisms such as central password and policy servers using Active Directory servers, we deploy them behind unidirectional gateways, rather than having SCADA systems trust IT controllers. Most commonly, we deploy one such server per plant.

Organized Crime

Working down the list of threats from top to bottom, we come to high-volume, indiscriminately-targeted malware produced by organized crime. With unidirectional gateways preventing any online transfer of malware into a SCADA system, the only method left by which such malware can enter the SCADA system is physical. We risk carrying such malware across a physical security perimeter in a cell phone, on a laptop, or on a USB drive. The usual solution to prevent such mechanisms from infecting a SCADA system is to deploy removable media and transient device controls.

Removable media controls are software and sometimes hardware that prevent USB, firewire, CD-ROM, DVD and other computer ports for removable media from allowing any file or content to be transferred via those ports or interfaces. Now, all software can be hacked, even device control software. The intent with device control systems is more educational, in preventing errors and omissions, than comprehensive deterrence of a determined, compromised insider.

Imagine connecting a cell phone to a USB port to charge, and seeing a message pop up on the computer saying, "Excuse me, what are you doing?" Seconds later all the video cameras in the room swing around to point at the offender, and a few seconds after that, the cell phone itself rings. The call is site security asking why the offender has just connected a removable device, full of who knows what malware, to the SCADA system.

Transient device controls are similar. The most common is called "Network Access Control" (NAC). Ethernet networks are the workhorse of modern networking in almost all SCADA networks, and every Ethernet device, laptops included, have a Media Access Control (MAC) Ethernet address. NAC-capable network switches can be configured to raise an alert when a device with an unrecognized MAC address is connected, and can be configured to block communications with such devices until an administrator authorizes the device. NAC can be defeated by a determined adversary but again, the primary purpose here is educational, and the prevention of errors and omissions.

Again – imagine a vendor visiting a SCADA site and connecting an unauthorized laptop to a SCADA network. Seconds later, every video camera swings around. Physical security personnel show up minutes later to escort the vendor off the property for having violated a safety (security) rule. The vendor is photographed and the photograph is mounted on the "wall of shame" at every entrance to the facility. A message below the photograph shows the vendor's name, and shows how long the vendor is banned from the facility. Word spreads quickly with a system like this, especially when all vendor and services contracts include a clause making the vendor liable for all costs and delays incurred because of these violations.

Removable media screening stations are deployed as well, as part of removable media controls. When information, such as antivirus signatures, must come into a SCADA site from time to time, that information must be subjected to the highest levels of scrutiny. All such information should at minimum pass through a removable media screening station, where the information is examined by a number of antivirus, sandboxing, whitelisting and other screening systems.

Effective media control and transient device control systems quickly teach our workers about the threat such media and devices pose to our SCADA systems. The systems block almost all of the flow of information from such media and devices into our SCADA systems from almost all well-meaning and even many malicious insiders.

Corporate Insiders

Last, consider the threat posed by corporate insiders, sipping coffee in an office building on another continent. Again though, this is just another kind of remote threat, and all such have been eliminated by the unidirectional gateways.

Secondary Measures

This intrusion prevention-centric discipline has none of the very labor-intensive, costly components in the IT-centric bottom-up defense-in-depth design.

Note that we are not saying do away with encryption, anti-malware, patching, passwords and intrusion detection altogether. What we are saying is that these security measures and systems should be secondary measures, not primary ones. Primary measures address the principle risk of intrusion, by preventing intrusions. Secondary measures acknowledge that no security system is perfect, and that people make mistakes. Secondary measures address residual risk due to errors and omissions.

This means we can and should scale our investment in these very costly secondary programs to reflect the small, residual risk reduction they buy us. For example:

- Whitelisting can be deployed on SCADA equipment that tolerates the technology. Whitelisting addresses the residual risks of malware that may be introduced to SCADA equipment through compromised product-vendor and services-vendor software updates or compromised software upgrades. Unlike antivirus scanners, whitelisting systems generally do not need to carry out periodic scans, and have been shown to be a better fit for SCADA security needs than antivirus systems. Whitelisting is far from perfect[6] [31] but can be a valuable secondary defense.
- Antivirus systems can still be deployed on equipment that does not need to run 24x7.
- Every SCADA site should still have some sort of patch program, because we really should eliminate what software and product vulnerabilities we can over time. Unlike IT programs though, the SCADA patching program is far from our first line of defense, and so can be scaled to address the residual risk of errors and omissions. In short, we should patch when we can afford to do so, not in a mad, costly panic to "stay ahead of the bad guys."

---

[6] Whitelisting can also be defeated by subverting software update mechanisms, as was done with the Flame attack in the wild [35].

- Encryption should be deployed across all WAN connections, and within the SCADA system, wherever practical. Our primary cyber and physical defenses should be more than capable of preventing malware and infected computers from being connected to our SCADA networks. However, in the rare case where something slips through, encryption helps slow the propagation of some kinds of attacks.

- Every SCADA site should still have an IDS and a security information and event management system (SIEM). Those systems though, can be tuned much more liberally than they are tuned on IT networks. The most useful thing a SCADA network IDS does is detect and alert on unrecognized network addresses and unauthorized equipment. This task can be carried out with almost no false alarms and the associated costly investigations of such alarms.

- Every SCADA site should still have a practiced incident response team. Again though, on a SCADA system defended as described above, these people will have little to do most of the time. That we have to invent attack scenarios as training for these people is a clear indication that we have moved from a detection-centric, reactive security posture to a sound, prevention-centric posture.

Summary

In short, preventing compromise is the key. Almost every SCADA system should reliably defeat essentially all those attacks that are less capable than the most sophisticated, military-grade assault.

Primary, preventive, physical and cyber-perimeter security controls should be the focus of most of our spending and attention, and must be focused on preventing intrusion. A strong primary, preventive security program eliminates almost all risk of attack from even sophisticated adversaries. Secondary controls deal with residual risk, and include detective controls and incident response capabilities. We can and should deploy secondary controls to deal with inevitable, but rare, errors and omissions in the application of our primary controls. We can and should however, scale the investment on these secondary controls to reflect the very small residual risk reduction these controls yield.

Even more briefly, modest amounts of money and effort spent on preventive measures, rather than IT-style detective and reactive measures, dramatically reduce the operating costs of security programs, and dramatically reduce the risk of SCADA system compromise as well.

Recommended Reading

Industrial Network Security, 2015, Eric Knapp and Joel Langill

SCADA Security

"Air gaps are unicorns, and provide a false sense of security,
so we need to put firewalls everywhere.

But firewalls are porous and also provide a false sense of security.
For that matter, every security technology has limitations.

So to avoid a false sense of security, we need to put every bit
of our SCADA system on the Internet with no protection whatsoever.

No, wait ... that's stupid."

-- *<name withheld by request>, 2014*

Chapter 6 – Unidirectional Gateways

Of all the security technologies discussed thus far, unidirectional gateways are the technology that IT gurus understand least, and so we include a brief introduction here. As with any technology, there are differences between versions and between vendors. In this chapter, we explore what the SCADA industry currently regards as the "gold standard" for unidirectional communications.

Unidirectional gateways are a technology that connects networks at very different levels of criticality[7], most often connecting safety-critical or reliability-critical SCADA networks to Internet-exposed corporate networks. The gateway technology is a combination of hardware and software. The unidirectional nature of the hardware makes the gateways secure, and the software moves the data. In many circumstances, the combination of hardware and software makes the gateways plug-and-play replacements for network firewalls.

Unidirectional Hardware

Unidirectional gateway hardware has two modules connected by a short fibre-optic cable[8,9]. The transmit (TX) module has a fibre-optic transmitter

---

[7] See Chapter 13 for a deeper discussion of network criticality.

[8] The fibre-optic cable in a unidirectional gateway is always short – generally between a half-meter and several hundred meters long. The entire gateway, including all hardware, software and the fibre, is always deployed entirely within the physical security perimeter of the protected facility. The most common deployment is within a single server rack.

[9] Fibre-optic connections are widely seen as superior to electric connections for unidirectional gateways. All electric circuits are circular after all, and it is difficult

– a laser – but no receiver. The RX module has a fibre-optic receiver – a photocell – but has no transmitter. A standard fibre-optic transceiver contains both a laser and a photocell. Unidirectional gateways do not use such transceivers[10]. The TX module can transmit light and signals to the RX module, but the RX module physically has no way to send anything back to the TX module.

In the most common deployment, the gateway is oriented to transmit information *out* of the SCADA network into the IT network, but is physically unable to send any message, any attack, or any information at all back into the SCADA network. When such a unidirectional gateway is the only connection between a SCADA network and any external network, information can leave the SCADA network, but there is no way any external message or information can be sent back into the SCADA network. All attacks are encoded in information, and with no way to send information into the SCADA network through a unidirectional gateway, there is no way to send an attack into the network through the gateway either.

No remote network attack and no remote control attack are possible from the destination of a unidirectionally-protected network. No remote misoperation is possible either, and no remote triggering of manually-implanted malware.

Server Replication and Device Emulation

The software part of a unidirectional gateway is called a "connector." A connector gathers information from industrial systems and uses that information to replicate servers and emulate devices. For example, in a power plant, all useful industrial data might be aggregated in a plant historian database. Anyone in the plant who needs access to the

---

or impossible to prove that no information can be encoded in returning electrons and voltages.

[10] Note that high-quality unidirectional gateway hardware typically has additional layers of protection – the laser/photocell difference is only the simplest layer of unidirectionality. For example, unidirectional optical cabling may be external, between physically separate TX and RX modules, to simplify audits and inspections, and TX and RX modules may have physically separate cabinets, power supplies, and even electrical grounding. Some unidirectional gateways may also be deployable with TX and RX components deployed some distance from each other, to frustrate the exotic attacks described in Chapter 13.

information can ask the database and get an answer. This is a common design in many industries, used to minimize data management and access costs.

In this example, an enterprise historian database has been deployed on the IT network, aggregating information from all of the power plants in the business. Again, this is a common design. Unidirectional gateway software synchronizes the contents of each plant historian to the enterprise historian. One such replication is illustrated in Figure (2).

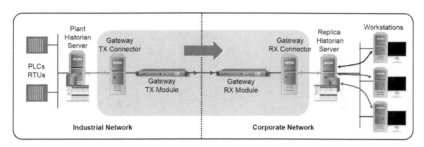

Figure (2) Unidirectional historian replication

In this example, the gateway's TX connector software runs on a computer connected to the SCADA network. The connector software is a normal client of the plant historian database, the same way that a spreadsheet is a client of a relational database. The connector software logs into the historian database and asks the database for the data which is to be sent to the enterprise network. This data is sent across the unidirectional hardware to the gateway's RX connector software, which is running on a computer connected to the corporate IT network.

The unidirectional gateway's RX connector software is a normal client of the enterprise historian. The software logs in to the enterprise historian and inserts the received data into that database. This process continues, second by second. In short, the unidirectional gateway maintains, in the enterprise historian, a faithful, real-time replica of the plant historian's data. Any program or user on the corporate network that needs real-time data can now ask the enterprise/replica historian on the IT network for that data, and be confident of receiving the same answer that the plant historian would have provided. No query, no acknowledgement, and no information at all is returned to the industrial network. Every bit of information can constitute an attack, so unidirectional gateways permit no information at all in the reverse direction.

In addition to replicating servers, unidirectional gateways can emulate devices. An OPC server is a very common device on SCADA networks. OPC servers provide a standard interface to access a wide variety of proprietary SCADA system hardware, software and communications protocols. Unidirectional OPC device emulation is illustrated in Figure (3).

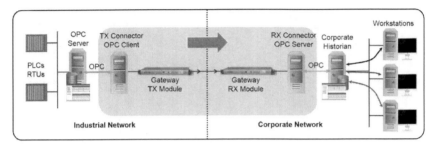

Figure (3): OPC device emulation

In the figure, the TX connector software is a standard OPC client. The connector software polls the OPC server for new information, typically once per second, and sends that information through the gateway hardware to the RX connector. On the corporate network, the RX connector emulates the SCADA system's OPC server. Any corporate system that needs real-time data, such as the enterprise historian database, can poll the gateway's replica OPC server for the data. The replica OPC server responds to queries in the same way as the industrial OPC server would have responded.

The existence of the replicas on the corporate network means that nobody and nothing ever needs to send a poll message, database query or other data request back into the SCADA network to retrieve any data. All of the data that anyone is authorized to retrieve is already available on the corporate network in some sort of replica database or emulated device.

If there is a problem on the corporate network, such as a serious security incident erasing a great many hard drives, the plant continues unaffected. The TX parts of a true unidirectional gateway send "blind" – they have no idea that chaos has taken hold of the corporate network. Hours, days or weeks later, when order has been restored on the corporate network, corporate IT can call the plant, ask them to click on a few buttons on the gateway's user interface, and retransmit and fill in any data gaps that may have arisen in the corporate historian's records.

No Traffic Forwarding

There is another important difference between firewalls and unidirectional gateways. When discussing the gateways, the question often arises: "what happens if the TX connector inside the SCADA system receives an unexpected message?" The motive for the question is modern malware that connects from compromised equipment to an Internet command and control center for instructions. If a SCADA system is compromised by such malware, could the malware reach out through a unidirectional gateway to send information to the Internet?

The answer most people expect has something to do with rules and configurations. Firewall vendors provide such answers. If a firewall receives any message, expected or not, then the firewall looks at the configured filter rules. If the message matches a rule, the firewall does what the rule says to do – the firewall generally either forwards the message, or drops it.

A unidirectional gateway though, is not a firewall and is not a router. Unidirectional gateways do not forward message traffic. The unidirectional hardware modules are physically connected to the computers running the connector software, as illustrated in Figures (2) and (3). There is no way to interact with the unidirectional hardware except through those two computers.

Each of these computers is a host – a source and a destination endpoint for IP messages, not a router. What happens when any host receives a message it does not expect? Say for example that the host receives a message containing a request to connect to the web server on "hackers-r-us.com." This message might be sent to the host from some piece of malware on a network to which the host is connected.

The gateway connector host is not a firewall, or a router. The host is also not a web server. It is certainly not "hackers-r-us.com." In short, there is nothing useful the host can do with that connect-request message. The host therefore throws the message away. This is not because there is a rule saying to throw the message away. The host throws the message away because there is nothing else it can reasonably do with the message.

Firewall experts can find this confusing. Unidirectional gateways clearly send *something* from one network to another. In what sense is this "something" not message traffic?

For the technically inclined, the TX connector host uses normal IP messaging to acquire a snapshot of application-layer state information from some application on the SCADA network. It is the state information that is transferred to the RX side of the gateway, not any of the IP messages used to acquire the information. Unidirectional gateways never forward messages received from the source / SCADA network.

This means that if common malware somehow gets a foothold inside a SCADA network, the malware cannot "phone home" through a unidirectional gateway. Neither will any packet from the TX network ever reach equipment on the RX network. This means no packet-level buffer-overflow, fuzzing or other attacks can be transmitted from equipment on the TX network to equipment on the RX network.

All of these are secondary benefits of deploying unidirectional gateways rather than firewalls.

Unidirectional FLIP

"But," the IT guys say, "what if we *need* to send something into a control system? Antivirus signatures for example, or batch production orders into a chemical plant?" This is a legitimate question. SCADA systems that require occasional remote inputs can use a unidirectional flip.

A flip is a kind of unidirectional gateway whose orientation can reverse periodically[11]. A flip is a combination of hardware and software. The flip hardware contains a single TX module, a single RX module and a short fibre-optic cable, just like a unidirectional gateway. A flip has only one TX module and one RX module in it, meaning it can send information in only one direction. This means that a flip is a *kind of* unidirectional gateway.

Which way does the flip transmit though? There is often a button or physical lock on the front panel of a flip unit. When the button is pressed, or key is inserted into the lock and turned, the flip behaves as if it had been physically picked up, turned over, and set down again. The unidirectional

---

[11] Unidirectional flip technology is currently only available from one vendor, Waterfall Security Solutions.

orientation of the flip reverses. A flip can be one-way out, or one-way in, but never both at the same time. That said, while a physical button or key may illustrate the concept of reversing unidirectional orientation, these physical mechanisms tend to be used only rarely. Most commonly, flip units reverse orientation on a site-defined schedule. A common example is periodic transmission of antivirus signatures, security updates and batch-plant production orders into SCADA systems.

For example, a flip might be configured to be oriented from a chemical plant control network out to a corporate network routinely. The flip might be configured though, to reverse orientation for ten minutes, at both 2:00 AM and 2:00 PM. When the flip reverses orientation, the gateway TX connector software on the corporate network wakes up. The antivirus connector reaches out to the Internet, pulls the latest antivirus signatures, inspects the signatures to ensure that they are authentic, and sends the signatures through the flip hardware into the SCADA network. On the inside, the RX connector software repeats the integrity checks and sends the signatures to the plant's AV server.

In addition, on the corporate network, the flip's TX Enterprise Resource Planning (ERP) connector reaches out to the corporate ERP system, pulls all of the batch production orders that have built up since the last flip, checks those orders for legitimacy, and sends them through the flip hardware into the SCADA system.

After ten minutes, the flip reverses again, back to an outbound orientation with respect to the SCADA system.

The flip technology provides a way to send many kinds of information into a protected control system network, while defeating the interactive remote control attack patterns that have proven so very effective against both IT and SCADA networks this last decade. Remote control attacks send queries into compromised networks, and see responses back. These attackers operate remote, compromised equipment continuously for days or weeks, learning enough about the target network to misoperate that network to maximum effect. Unidirectional flip technology reverses only on a schedule, usually at long intervals. This dramatically slows down remote control attacks, increasing our opportunity to detect and remediate them.

Furthermore, since a unidirectional flip is a kind of unidirectional gateway, a flip does not forward messages either. This means that unlike firewalls, attacks such as buffer-overflows or fuzzing attacks embedded in the primitive structure of messages cannot pass through a flip.

In all cases though, whether via the flip or removable media, all information passing into a SCADA network should receive the highest levels of scrutiny. For example, cryptographic vendor signatures should be verified on anti-virus signatures and security updates before using those updates, and batch or other instructions should be examined to ensure they contain "reasonable" instructions for the physical, industrial system.

The flip raises the bar for cyber security. No hacker sipping coffee on another continent should be able to reach into our most important control systems and manipulate those systems at will. The flip specifically defeats the kind of interactive remote control that the world's most advanced attackers use to defeat IT-class protections.

Inbound/Outbound Gateways

What do we do if we need information sent continuously into a SCADA network? For example, a power-grid control center might need to monitor the power output of a generator every second or two. The control center might also need to send new instructions to that generator every second or two, saying "produce more power" or "produce less power" as part of the process of matching generated power to the second-by-second power consumption of the grid.

In these cases, we can set up a unidirectional gateway to replicate servers from the power plant to the grid control center, and we can set up a second, independent gateway to replicate servers from the grid control center into the power plant. This combination is known as a set of inbound/outbound unidirectional gateways.

Note that inbound/outbound gateways do not forward messages. In our example, grid control centers use the Inter-Control-Center Protocol (ICCP) to communicate with power plants. In this example, the inbound/outbound gateways do not forward ICCP messages from control centers to the power plant, or forward responses back to the control center. Unidirectional gateways always replicate servers or emulate devices.

In the ICCP example, the inbound gateway software polls the control center ICCP server. The gateway software also creates an ICCP emulator inside the SCADA network for the generator control system to poll. Similarly, the outbound gateway polls the generator's ICCP server, and creates an ICCP emulator outside the SCADA network for the control center to poll. These two gateway systems are completely independent. In practice, they are most often set up on different network segments, so that software elements of the two gateway solutions cannot exchange messages with each other.

Again, the big difference security-wise between an inbound/outbound gateway configuration and a firewall is that firewalls forward messages. To attack our power plant's ICCP server through the firewall, our enemies need only to launch an attack packet – say an ICCP buffer overflow attack – through the firewall. If our enemy has chosen the attack packet carefully, the firewall will not detect that it is an attack, because it looks too much like a normal ICCP packet. In this case, the firewall forwards the attack right into the power plant's SCADA network. The attacker now has their code running in the ICCP server in the plant's SCADA network, and can work to pivot deeper into the network to damage equipment at the plant.

In an inbound/outbound gateway configuration, the outbound gateway hardware is unable to send any attack, or any information at all, back into our protected power plant. The only network attack possibility open to our enemy is via the inbound gateway.

The inbound gateway software does not forward messages. To attack the SCADA systems in the power plant, our enemy must compromise both the TX computer that is part of the inbound gateway configuration and the RX computer. The compromised RX computer however, is unable to return any information, intelligence or feedback to the attacker. In practice, devising an attack to reach deeper into the SCADA network is possible only with insider assistance at the targeted site. An attack through an inbound gateway is therefore at least a three-step exercise, requiring insider assistance.

In contrast, an attack through a firewall is generally a one-step exercise, with feedback immediately available as to whether the attack worked and what the rest of the SCADA system looks like.

Application Data Control

Application data control (ADC) is policy-based control over data in motion through unidirectional gateways. Firewall-based "deep packet inspection" provides some of the features of application data control, but only for IT communications, as well as a very small number of OT

59

industrial protocols. Unidirectional application data control is available for a wide variety of industrial protocols.

When a unidirectional gateway requests data from a server, the gateway can see what data items and data types are returned. The gateway assigns a unique name to each data item, and activates the ADC policy engine. The engine can be configured to permit certain names or values to pass through the gateway, be dropped by the gateway, be edited by the gateway before being forwarded, or have other actions applied. ADC software runs on a host running the unidirectional gateway connector software – on either the SCADA side of the gateway, the external side, or both.

For example, each value whose history is tracked in process historians is identified with a unique "tag name." An ADC instance might be configured to permit certain tag names to pass from the SCADA system to a corporate network, but not to pass others. The forbidden names might represent trade secrets or other confidential information that should not be made available on the external network. In another example, a gateway might be configured to replicate part of a SQLServer database from a corporate network to a SCADA network. The ADC instance could then be configured to permit certain tables to pass, and not others. The instance could also be configured to take all large "blob" data items, write them to the filesystem, scan them with a number of antivirus engines, and pass them on into the SCADA system only if all of the scans report that the data is clean.

Using Unidirectional Gateways

Unidirectional gateways are generally deployed to replace one layer of firewalls in a layered network architecture. For example, Figure (4) illustrates a typical self-contained physical plant, with one or more DCS-style local control systems. The most common layer of firewalls to replace is at the boundary between the plant-wide operations network, and the plant-wide corporate network, as illustrated.

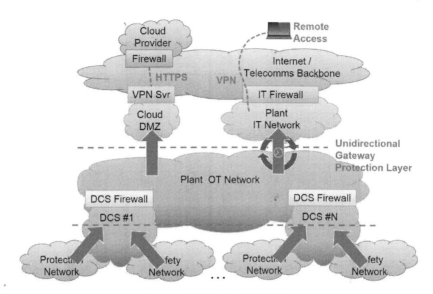

Figure (4) Typical DCS Site

In the diagram, the large arrows are complete unidirectional gateways, including two hosts running TX and RX connector software, as well as the TX and RX unidirectional hardware modules and cabling. The large arrow with rotation icons is a unidirectional flip.

The most common outward-oriented, industrial replication at this "IT/OT" interface layer is either some kind of plant historian replication or some kind of industrial device replication using one of the many OPC protocol variants, and a host of secondary replications. Secondary replications often include file server replication for routine file transfers, syslog and other security protocol replications to a Security Operations Center (SOC), and Simple Network Management Protocol (SNMP) replications to a Network Operations Center (NOC). Inbound replications generally include antivirus signatures, security updates, batch recipes, production orders, and industry-specific coordination with customers and suppliers.

In DCS-style plants, unidirectional gateways may also be deployed at the boundary between safety or protection networks and the DCS network, or at the boundary between the DCS and the plant network. For safety and protection networks, the gateways enable continuous monitoring of those important networks without introducing any risk of information or attacks flowing into those networks.

Gateways at the DCS/plant-network boundary are becoming more common, especially in the North American power grid. Provisions in the North American Electric Reliability Corporation Critical Infrastructure Protection (NERC CIP) Version 5 regulations reward power plants with major reductions in cyber-security regulatory requirements if plants "segment" their SCADA systems [32]. A segmented plant is one where no compromise of one generating unit is able to affect any other generating units within 15 minutes of the original compromise. Such guarantees are possible when generating unit DCSs are protected unidirectionally, but not with firewalls.

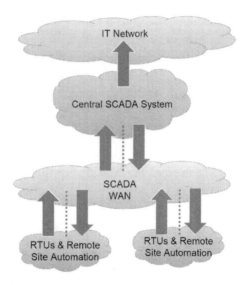

Figure (5): Unidirectional SCADA/WAN design

Figure (5) illustrates a typical unidirectional SCADA system design for WAN-centric SCADA system designs, such as are used in electric transmission and distribution systems, pipelines, water systems, and railways. In the diagram, each large arrow is a full unidirectional gateway. The dashed line between gateways indicates that inbound and outbound gateways represent independent replications, and do not communicate with or coordinate with each other at all.

The WAN-centric design of Figure (5) represents a distributed system that is more difficult to secure than the DCS-style plant in Figure (4). The difficulty is due to the existence of the WAN and the many physically distributed substations, pumping stations and other sites connected to the WAN.

The problem is that the physical infrastructure of the WAN – wiring, fibre, microwave components, and routers – generally extends well outside of the physical perimeter of any industrial site managed by the owner/operator of the SCADA system. An attacker who physically breaks into one of these distant, unstaffed sites is in a position to connect a laptop or other attack computer physically into WAN connections at the site. This generally permits the attacker to affect not only the site she has broken into, but all of the sites on the WAN, including the central SCADA site.

Gaining access to the SCADA WAN is even more straightforward when distant sites are not physically protected, but are merely isolated devices in physically exposed locations. Such devices are typical of the Industrial Internet of Things. We defer discussion of that topic until Chapter 12.

In distributed, SCADA-WAN networks, unidirectional gateways are generally deployed in up to three network boundaries in the network architecture. A gateway may be deployed at the boundary between the central SCADA system and the corporate network – this is very similar in kind and motivation to the most common unidirectional gateway deployments in the DCS-style plants illustrated in Figure (4). A gateway may also be deployed at the control center / WAN interface, to protect the control center from attacks originating in the WAN, or in distant sites. When deployed at distant sites, each gateway protects the site – the substation, the pumping station, etc. – where the gateway is physically deployed.

The most common deployment in an unstaffed site sees inbound/outbound unidirectional gateways deployed at the site's WAN connection, replicating the devices at the site to the central SCADA system across a VPN connection, and replicating the central site to the unstaffed site. This design permits remote control of the unstaffed site, as well as monitoring. Flip units and outbound-only gateways are deployed at this WAN interface as well, though less commonly.

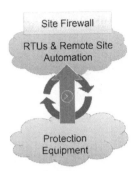

Figure (6): Protecting protection equipment

The second most popular type of deployment at distant, unstaffed sites protects safety and protection networks at these sites, as illustrated in Figure (6). This design uses a firewall at the site's WAN interface, with a conventional VPN connection to the central SCADA site, and provides strong protection for safety and protection equipment. In this design, a cyber attack can still cause short-term outages of the physical process. Remote attackers however, will find it nearly impossible to cause injuries, environmental damage, or long-lasting equipment damage, because of the protections the gateway equipment provides to safety and equipment protection devices.

Summary

Unidirectional gateways replicate industrial servers, and emulate industrial devices, through unidirectional hardware. Unidirectional gateways are not routers, and never forward IP messages or any other traffic from an industrial network to an external network, or vice-versa. Unidirectional gateways permit external applications and users to monitor safety-critical and reliability-critical control systems, without introducing any risk of remote control or unauthorized operation.

When remote control information simply must flow into a SCADA network from outside, variants of unidirectional gateways can facilitate such flows without the worst risks that always accompany firewall deployments. A unidirectional flip can send information into a protected network on a schedule. Inbound/outbound unidirectional gateways can provide continuous information flows. Both reliably defeat the interactive remote control attacks so favored by hacktivists and intelligence agencies. Application data control can provide an extra layer of protection.

Unidirectional gateways are most often deployed to replace one layer of firewalls in a classic defense-in-depth network architecture, thus breaking the flow of infection and remote control from the Internet, or some other WAN, into protected SCADA networks.

The most modern SCADA security standards either recommend or require unidirectional gateways for connections between networks at different levels of criticality [25]. Examples of such networks include connections between safety systems and control systems, between any site and a WAN, and between control networks and corporate networks. Within critical network segments, firewalls may still be used for internal segmentation to address residual risks such as certain kinds of unsophisticated attacks by SCADA insiders, while still permitting liberal two-way communications between internal control system components. Firewalls however, are not considered effective for protecting connections that cross network-criticality boundaries.

Generally speaking, the world will be measurably safer when more unidirectional security gateways are deployed to protect SCADA networks.

Recommended Reading

Cyber-Physical Security: Protecting Critical Infrastructure at the State and Local Level, 2017 Edition, by Robert M. Clark and Simon Hakim

"Stuxnet is a stone
thrown by people who live in a glass house."

-- Marcus Ranum,
Fabius Maximus blog, 2012

Chapter 7 – Stuxnet Case Study

For many SCADA security practitioners, the test used to measure any security program or security technology is the Stuxnet worm. "Will approach/technology X stop the next Stuxnet worm?" we all ask. This is the wrong question. That said, there is value in comparing both Chapter 4's IT-centric defense-in-depth approach and Chapter 5's top-down, preventive approach to the case of Stuxnet, not least to understand why "will X stop the next Stuxnet?" is the wrong question.

Some background: for anyone who has not heard, the Stuxnet worm is the malware credited with destroying about 1000 uranium enrichment centrifuges in Iran's nuclear program in 2010 [33]. No-one has officially laid claim to Stuxnet, but there is widespread speculation and "reports from anonymous sources" that the malware was produced as a cooperation between U.S. military and Israeli intelligence agencies. For months, the worm carried out its mission, undetected by antivirus systems, intrusion detection systems, intrusion prevention systems, or any other cyber-security mechanism. The Symantec team who produced a detailed analysis of the worm described it as "the most sophisticated" they had ever seen [34].

The worm was certainly unprecedented in terms of the damage it caused[12]. The Stuxnet worm was based on a detailed knowledge of the design of the physical systems, control systems and security systems at a single target: the Natanz uranium enrichment site[13]. Once released in the

---

[12] Reports of earlier SCADA-system attacks with greater physical impact have all been discredited. For example, a report discrediting claims that CIA sabotage in 1982 destroyed a Siberian natural gas pipeline in "the largest man-made, non-nuclear explosion to date," is available at [57].

[13] Reports that a Stuxnet-like cyber attack on Iran's Fordow uranium enrichment site caused a massive explosion killing hundreds of people have also been discredited [58].

uranium-enrichment control system, the worm carried out its destructive mission autonomously, without any of the remote control that less-sophisticated attacks depend on.

The worm was unprecedented in terms of its complexity as well. The Stuxnet worm used known, poorly known and unknown "zero-day" vulnerabilities to carry out its mission. The worm used encryption keys apparently stolen from well-known equipment manufacturers to help install essential components of itself on compromised systems. The worm moved between physical sites on USB drives, moved within sites across networks and through firewalls, disabled antivirus systems and was invisible to most intrusion detection and other security systems. Study of historical antivirus archives and other records indicate that versions of the worm carried out their mission almost completely invisibly for twelve months before coming to public attention.

Security Technology Nonsense

Much has been written about Stuxnet, and much of what has been written is nonsense[14]. Many authors took a copy of the Stuxnet worm and tested it against a variety of defensive technologies. During the time that the worm "flew under the radar," there were no AV signatures for it, and so antivirus systems were not able detect the worm. Whitelisting/application control systems could detect Stuxnet though, even without signatures, and so many authors concluded that whitelisting systems must be a more effective protection against the next Stuxnet-class attack than antivirus systems. People tested the worm against different sorts of intrusion detection systems as well. They concluded that when one kind could detect the worm, and the other kind could not, the first system must be more effective than the second.

This was, and is, all nonsense.

The circumstantial evidence of the Stuxnet worm's design suggests that the worm was designed using a detailed knowledge of its target. The worm was designed to destroy uranium centrifuges at the Natanz target, and appears designed to defeat security systems at Natanz and at one of the Natanz contractors' sites as well. The contractor site was presumably defended less-heavily than the Natanz site, and so was easier to

---

[14] Including many articles written by this author.

compromise. Once in control of contractor computers, the worm could be embedded in control-system project files and carried into the uranium enrichment site on USB drives and CD-ROMs.

Stuxnet's authors most likely knew that no online path between the Internet and the uranium-enrichment control system existed, and so made the worm able to propagate across USB drives and Siemens S7 project files. The worm's authors most likely knew that antivirus systems were deployed at the site, and tested the worm against those systems to make sure none of them detected the worm. The same holds true for intrusion detection systems.

Why then, did whitelisting stop the worm when researchers tested the worm against such systems? Whitelisting can certainly be defeated [31]. Whitelisting can also be defeated by subverting software update mechanisms, as was done with the Flame attack in the wild [35]. The most likely reason Stuxnet did not include mechanisms to defeat whitelisting is that there were no whitelisting protections deployed at Stuxnet's target in Iran. If no whitelisting was deployed, there was no need to build anti-whitelisting techniques into an already-costly, already-complex weapon.

The same holds true for intrusion detection systems. If Stuxnet's authors knew which systems were deployed at Natanz and at contractor sites, there was no reason to make the worm undetectable by all of the world's intrusion detection systems. The authors needed only to test the worm against the deployed defenses and ensure that the worm was sufficiently masked to defeat specifically those defenses. That one security technology or another would have defeated Stuxnet while it flew under the radar is not a reflection of the strength of any of those technologies, but rather a reflection of what technologies were and were not deployed at Stuxnet's targets.

Nothing Is "Secure"

All of this really is a consequence of the first law of cyber security: nothing is secure. When our enemy knows exactly how our systems are built and how they are defended, and when that enemy has enough money and skill to build an attack that can defeat every one of our defenses, we do not have a cyber-security problem. There is no cyber-security technology we can deploy to defeat that enemy with a high degree of confidence. What we have instead, is an espionage problem. We need to identify which of our people are cooperating with our enemies, both actively and inadvertently. We need to stop the flow of information to our enemies so that they are no longer able to craft attacks specific to our defenses. Only when this is accomplished will we have any chance of designing new defenses able to defeat our enemies' future cyber weapons.

So again, the question everyone wants answered is "how do we defeat the next Stuxnet?" That is: how do we build a defensive system so capable that we reliably defeat even those adversaries with essentially unlimited cyber and physical resources? That question has no answer, because nothing is secure. Many authors, however, have ignored this reality and published a great deal of nonsensical advice.

Firewall Advice And Other Nonsense

One bit of nonsense has been accepted as true by a dangerously large number of industrial sites – many authors advised forbidding all use of USB drives, and deploying firewalls as the only means of exchanging information with SCADA systems. The reasoning is that since Stuxnet spread on USB keys, gluing USB ports and CD drives shut will prevent compromise by "the next Stuxnet." Firewalls are then necessary to communicate any routinely-needed updates into SCADA systems, such as antivirus signatures, intrusion detection signatures, new security updates, and new SCADA configurations.

These authors and the sites who mistakenly believe them ignore the facts. Yes, Stuxnet was carried between sites on USB keys and in Siemens project files, but the worm also propagated within sites across networks and through firewalls, including IT/OT firewalls [36]. To prevent compromise by gluing ports shut then, we would need to glue shut all of the USB ports on all computers and laptops on the corporate IT network as well. In addition, since Stuxnet spread from the contractor site in Siemens project files, none of these measures at the target site would have prevented infection, since the contractor would inevitably have found some way to move the new, improved – and infected – SCADA project files into the live SCADA system.

Other nonsense advice included advice to control-system vendors to fix "the next Stuxnet" problem by making whitelisting systems integral to their control system product offerings. This ignored the fact that whitelisting systems can be broken, and that Stuxnet almost certainly did not defeat whitelisting systems only because there was no whitelisting deployed at the worm's target. Certain anomaly-based intrusion detection systems were able to detect the Stuxnet worm, and those systems' vendors persuaded many sites to deploy such intrusion detection systems. This ignored the fact that anomaly-based systems can be deceived as well, and presumably Stuxnet would have carried out such deception were it necessary to compromise Natanz or the contractor site.

Stopping "The Next Stuxnet"

With this background, we compare the tactics recommended in Chapters 4 and 5 to "the next Stuxnet."

"The next Stuxnet" can mean many things. If by "the next Stuxnet" we mean the next minor change to the existing Stuxnet worm, never fear. All antivirus vendors have issued signatures to identify all public variants of the Stuxnet worm and minor variations thereof. The classic IT-centric defense-in-depth approach in Chapter 4 advises us to put antivirus systems everywhere possible, and this tactic will catch the existing Stuxnet worm. The preventive approach in Chapter 5 advises us to scan removable media with antivirus systems and other technologies before permitting such media through our physical perimeters, and to deploy antivirus systems on all computers where such deployment is practical. Both of these processes will catch the existing Stuxnet worm.

If by "the next Stuxnet," we mean the next attack, whatever its nature, from an adversary as capable as the authors of the Stuxnet worm, then we have a more interesting question. If we were defended by a Chapter 4's classic IT-centric security program, our adversary would never produce an enormously complex and costly weapon such as Stuxnet in the first place. With Chapter 4's defenses in place, our enemies can simply use one of the targeted remote-control attacks that routinely defeat IT-centric defense-in-depth programs.

If though, we are defended by Chapter 5's preventive approach, our enemy has little choice but to make the investment in a costly, complex autonomous weapon. By deploying a modern, prevention-focused security program, we eliminate the easy attack routes and force our enemies' hand into the most complex of attacks.

To create an autonomous weapon, our enemy is likely to first try what Stuxnet's authors are believed to have done, and go find one of our suppliers with a less effective security program than we have. On that supplier's network, our enemies can learn about our systems from the supplier's documentation and test-beds, and can infect the control system updates that our suppliers are preparing for us.

If our suppliers have all used Chapter 5's modern, prevention-based approach to protect their test beds, their development systems and any computer with access to documentation or technology destined for our site, then our enemy has an even harder problem. Now our enemy must find a way to steal the information they need, most likely by compromising one of our people or one of our suppliers' people who have access to the information. With this information, our enemy can create "the next Stuxnet" – an autonomous weapon able to defeat the security of our SCADA systems and any other intermediate systems needed to infect us.

In short, deploying Chapter 4's IT-centric, defense-in-depth, detective and reactive approach to security means nobody needs to write another Stuxnet to compromise us. Deploying Chapter 5's prevention-centric approach means our enemies have little choice but to invest in "the next Stuxnet" to come after us. Our best hope of defeating an enemy this capable is to deploy Chapter 5's unidirectional gateways, physical security and inspection mechanisms, and:

1) Involve our own national intelligence agencies in the process of ensuring that our suppliers and people are not compromised, that our security systems are state of the art, and

2) Deploy the best inspection technologies possible for all hardware, software, and other information passing through our perimeters – see Chapter 13 for examples.

In the worst case though, there is no reliable defense against "the next Stuxnet." Anyone who tells us otherwise is spouting nonsense, or selling something, or both. Detective, IT-centric security programs have a poor chance of defeating even the ubiquitous remote-control attacks, much less an attack as sophisticated as Stuxnet. Preventive, SCADA-centric security programs defeat remote control attacks reliably, and make life very hard for an enemy trying to compromise our systems.

There are no guarantees, but a perimeter-focused, state-of-the-art security program can make life arbitrarily difficult for our enemies. We can and should make our enemies come to tear their hair out and curse the names of our SCADA security designers.

Summary

Stuxnet was a military-grade attack on Iran's uranium enrichment program. Using the worm to evaluate the effectiveness of security technologies is nonsense – every defense can be defeated, and the worm was presumably designed to defeat only those defenses it needed to, in order to achieve its authors' mission objectives. Saying, "firewall everything and forbid USB drives" is pointless, because Stuxnet spread easily through firewalls within compromised organizations, as do remote control attacks.

There is no way to defeat military-grade attacks reliably. A strong prevention-focused SCADA security program though, can make compromise of our SCADA systems arbitrarily difficult for even military-grade adversaries.

Recommended Reading

Symantec W32.Stuxnet.Dossier Version 1.4, 2011, by Nicolas Falliere, Liam O Murchu, and Eric Chien

To Kill a Centrifuge – A Technical Analysis of What Stuxnet's Creators Tried to Achieve, 2013, by Ralph Langner

SCADA Security

"Entropy increases. Things fall apart."

-- John Green, Looking for Alaska, 2005

Chapter 8 – Security Programs

Strong, preventive security measures do little to prevent the compromise of SCADA networks connected to open Wi-Fi routers. There is also no point eliminating all such routers if six months later some well-meaning new employee connects yet another one to the SCADA network because the employee has received no security training. Worse, even if our security system is sound, cyber attacks only become more sophisticated over time. Attack tools evolve like any other mature software product for which there is a large market, which means our security technologies and procedures must continue to evolve as well.

SCADA Security programs are comprehensive systems that ensure not just an acceptable level of security for our SCADA systems today, but ensure that this level of security is maintained and is still acceptable over the course of time [37], [32], [38], [23]. Security programs are intended to address not only all aspects of cyber security and physical security for our SCADA systems, but require that we regularly re-evaluate the threat environment and re-evaluate SCADA security protections in light of that changing environment.

All currently-published frameworks have serious flaws.

The NIST Framework

Consider for example the U.S. National Institute of Standards and Technology (NIST) Framework for Improving Critical Infrastructure Cybersecurity [39]. This framework is typical of SCADA security programs, and the framework's flaws are typical of the flaws of almost all such programs. The NIST framework organizes security controls into five categories:

- Identify – identify who has the authority to make security decisions and spend security budgets within an organization, and establish security program policies, procedures and responsibilities. "Identify" activities also include understanding and inventorying threats, attack capabilities, physical and cyber targets of attacks, SCADA systems, security systems and every other kind of device on SCADA networks. This inventory should include physical network cabling, telephony cabling, and wireless spectrum in the vicinity of the physical process.

- Protect – take measures to prevent adverse outcomes. Protective measures include security technology deployments, such as unidirectional gateways and removable media controls. Protective measures also include training and awareness-raising measures to ensure that the people involved in designing, operating, maintaining, and securing SCADA systems each understand their role in the security program, both initially and as time passes.
- Detect – take measures to detect compromised systems and detect violations of security policies.
- Respond – develop measures to limit the impact of compromised systems. This generally includes trained and practiced incident response teams, as well as forensics capabilities to determine after the fact which systems and data may have been affected by a successful compromise.
- Recover – develop the ability to recover normal business operations after an attack. This generally includes a way to restore compromised equipment to a "clean" state after an attack.

In the NIST Framework, the "identify" function includes iteration. We are not "done" when we deploy a security system, because circumstances change. The NIST "identify" function includes periodic reassessments of and modifications to the security program in light of any changes in business need, threat environment, available technologies, budgets and other conditions.

The NIST Framework, like most frameworks, is good in that it provides an outline for all of the functions essential to a security program. Unlike IT security frameworks, the NIST Framework does make an effort to address not only IT-style critical infrastructures, such as search engines, trading systems and banking systems, but industrial critical infrastructures as well.

The NIST framework, like most frameworks though, is deficient by failing to make any distinction between primary and secondary security measures, and fails to point out how these measures differ between data-centric IT systems and safety/reliability/control-centric industrial and SCADA systems. NIST's entire program categories of Detect, Respond and Recover represent secondary priorities. Identify and Protect must always be the highest priorities for SCADA systems.

A subtler deficiency in the NIST framework is a lack of emphasis on physical security. All cyber-security frameworks contain some token acknowledgement of the importance of physical security, to a degree that is appropriate for IT networks. Most SCADA networks though, are protected by strong physical security perimeters, and should be protected by close-to-impenetrable network security perimeters. Members of the public must not be permitted to walk up to a high-voltage transformer while that transformer is in use. Anyone who can walk up to physical equipment can generally take physical measures to misoperate, disable, damage or otherwise impair the operation of that equipment. Unlike IT networks, both physical and cyber perimeter protections are and should always be the primary protections of choice on SCADA networks.

Maturity Models

The NIST Framework includes the concept of "implementation tiers" which are very similar to the more common concept of "organizational maturity models" [40]. Maturity models go hand-in-hand with security programs, and are among the most deceiving aspects of SCADA security programs. A cyber-security maturity model is intended to measure how capable an organization's cyber-security processes are. A high score on a maturity capability assessment is supposed to mean that an organization is able to secure its SCADA systems thoroughly and reliably.

The problem with capability maturity models is that there is no consensus as to what "secure SCADA systems adequately" means and so most maturity-model scores are worthless. More specifically, there is a decade-old, broad understanding that some IT protections are difficult to apply to SCADA systems. There is not, however, a broad understanding that IT-style security approaches are entirely inadequate to the needs of SCADA systems, that the IT-style emphasis on detective rather than protective measures misses the point, and that the security measures that are difficult to apply to SCADA systems really should be secondary measures rather than primary measures in the first place.

Most organizations apply IT approaches and technologies to SCADA security, and some organizations do so with a high degree of sophistication. When such organizations are assessed against capability maturity models, they generally receive high scores. Senior management concludes that they have "done the right thing" and that these high scores mean that the organization's SCADA systems are well-defended.

They are of course, mistaken.

SCADA systems in IT-centric organizations with high maturity model scores are roughly as secure as the best IT systems, which are generally much less secure than safety-critical and reliability-critical industrial processes need to be. SCADA systems protected with prevention-centric, perimeter-focused measures tend to be far less vulnerable to cyber assaults than SCADA systems with IT-centric protections, no matter the maturity score of the organization.

Maturity models measure the thoroughness of organizational security processes, not the strength of SCADA security systems.

Summary

Most SCADA security programs over-emphasize detection, response and recovery activities. While such activities may be essential to constantly-compromised IT networks, SCADA network security must focus instead on preventing compromise. Maturity models measure the strength of business processes used to manage a SCADA security program, not the strength of the program itself. As long as there is no consensus as to how to measure the strength of a SCADA security program, measuring the strength of business processes produces meaningless results.

Recommended Reading

Framework for Improving Critical Infrastructure Cybersecurity, Version 1.0, 2014, U.S. National Institute of Standards and Technology

Cybersecurity Capability Maturity Model (C2M2) Version 1.1, 2014, by U.S. Department of Energy and U.S. Department of Homeland Security

*"Informed decision-making
comes from a long tradition of guessing
and then blaming others for inadequate results."*

-- *Scott Adams, Cartoonist, (1957-)*

Chapter 9 – Risk Management and Governance

Boards of directors and other senior business decision makers have a fiduciary responsibility to manage risk, including cyber-risk [41]. If a high maturity model or implementation tier score does not reliably indicate that an organization is protecting SCADA systems adequately, and if IT-centric advice is used by a great many expert-class security teams to protect SCADA systems, then how can boards of directors or other senior executives possibly carry out their risk-management responsibilities? These business people almost never have the technical training needed to evaluate an organization's cyber security systems themselves, and the information they get from their executives can be seriously flawed.

Take for example a personal report from an inquisitive member of senior management at an electric utility. During a risk management meeting, the senior member asked the utility's CIO "What is the worst thing that could happen if an attacker were to gain access to the central SCADA systems?" The immediate answer was that the systems are protected and a successful attack was highly unlikely. Upon further questioning, answers over time ranged from no outage, to a cascading outage, which would likely damage some equipment. A cascading outage is one where overloaded components in the electric grid are automatically taken offline to prevent damage. This shifts electric loads to other parts of the grid, overloading those components and triggering further automatic shutdowns. The cycle repeats until a large fraction of the grid is offline. Throughout the ensuing discussion as to whether a cascading outage is the correct answer, the CIO maintained, "Don't worry, we are secure. That can't happen."

Since nothing is or ever can be "secure," this answer is, of course, nonsense.

In another example, senior cyber-security experts on a panel at a SCADA security conference in the oil and gas sector were heard to observe, in turn:

a) "Security is pure cost."
b) "There has to be an ROI for every one of our security investments, so we use a risk-based approach."
c) "Cyber risk calculations can't be quantitative, so we use a qualitative approach. This makes ROI calculations impossible."
d) "It's simpler than that – just never be the highest-ranked person to know about a risk. Always make your boss sign off on it."
e) "It all depends on the risk appetite of your board and executive."

The practice of cyber risk management and of corporate governance regarding cyber risks seems deeply confused.

Corporate governance regarding all types of risk starts with the responsibility of board members and executives to safeguard shareholder value in for-profit organizations, and to protect the public interest in public institutions. These business decision-makers are required to do so by addressing all risks appropriately. This is generally accomplished in the context of an organizational risk management program that considers risks of all types, including for example, hurricanes, flu pandemics, cyber assaults, terrorist attacks and outright warfare.

When considering risks, senior decision-makers must decide how to address each risk. The choice is generally one of mitigating, transferring, or accepting the risk. Mitigating the risk means taking action to reduce or eliminate the risk. Transferring the risk means paying a willing third party, such as an insurer, to reimburse the organization, should the risk ever be realized. Accepting the risk means deliberately doing nothing. This means we must then suffer the consequences should the risk ever be realized.

Since nothing can ever be perfectly safe, there must always be risks the business accepts. For example, most private corporations have no plan to mitigate or transfer the risk of a meteor striking the planet, one large enough to destroy all life on the planet.

Any risk a business chooses to accept is called "residual risk." The degree of residual risk to which an organization is exposed is a measure of how secure that organization is.

Quantitative Assessment

The most common way to assess risks in conventional risk management, for example risks such as floods and flu pandemics, is to calculate an annualized loss expectancy (ALE) for each type of risk:

$$ALE = \text{(probability of risk event(s) occurring this year)} \times \text{(cost of consequences should they occur)}$$

This approach works well for hurricanes and flu pandemics, because we have historical records showing how frequent and how severe such events are. This approach also works for high-frequency, low-impact (HFLI) cyber risks, again because we have statistics.

Take for example common virus/malware. Say for example, that 73 such compromises occurred in a large enterprise last year, and the cost of cleaning them out averaged $153,000 per compromise. Say also that we expect no significant changes in the threat environment or the defenses deployed this year, and so the expected cost to the business of this risk next year is 73 x $153,000 or roughly 11 million dollars. This $11M expected loss might be judged by senior decision-makers to be an acceptable risk, especially if a more-effective security system would cost much more than $11 million.

This backwards-looking approach works very badly for low-frequency, high-impact (LFHI) risks. How many times last year did a cyber attack cause a cascading outage of an electric grid, anywhere in the world? As far as anyone knows, no cyber attack has ever been responsible for such an outage. Does this mean the probability of such an attack and outage occurring next year is zero? The first law of cybersecurity says that nothing is secure. The probability of such an attack is therefore clearly not zero.

Worse, attacks and easily-available attack tools become more sophisticated every year. In the absence of new proactive measures to reduce risk, the risk of such an outage increases every year. Should we make up probabilities to feed into our ALE equation? Should our executives and board members be asked to make business decisions regarding serious risks based on fictional probabilities?

81

Qualitative Assessment

The standard response to this problem is exemplified very clearly in the French Agence nationale de la sécurité des systèmes d'information (ANSSI) standards for critical infrastructure security. The ANSSI standards use qualitative, not quantitative assessments [25]. Qualitative assessment calculations can be complex, but all involve a number of standard elements. Consider a simple, representative example where:

$$Risk = likelihood \; x \; threat \; x \; vulnerability \; x$$
$$consequences$$

We assign small whole numbers to each of these elements. For the cascading outage example we might say the likelihood of an attack is low (1) and the threat/capability of our enemies is moderate (3). Our defenses are good though, so we assess our vulnerability as (1). The consequences of such a widespread outage are serious though, so we assign the highest possible value to consequences (5). This means our overall qualitative risk score is 1 x 3 x 1 x 5 = 15. If the board set our maximum acceptable risk at 22, and 15 is less than 22, we accept this risk.

Really?

All qualitative calculations use numbers, and so these calculations have at least the appearance of scientific rigor. What does a risk threshold of 22 in this example mean though? In truth, even experts who carry out these qualitative analyses for a living are suspicious of this kind of calculation. The average board member is no such expert and will have a much less thorough understanding of the calculation and its fundamental limitations.

To start with, parts of the example calculation above are entirely subjective. Who says, "Our defenses are good so our vulnerability is (1)?" Give exactly the same SCADA security defensive posture to three different security experts, and we often see three entirely different assessments. For example, a penetration testing expert might say, "Click, click, click – I just broke in and took over the operator HMI by remote control. I can click on any button I wish and so misoperate the physical process. In short, there are straightforward attack paths through this system that lead to entirely unacceptable consequences. I rate the system's defensive posture as poor." An IT security risk expert might say, of exactly the same system, "This SCADA system is vulnerable to only those attacks to which our well-defended IT system is vulnerable. We routinely accept the risk of such attacks on our IT networks and so should accept those risks on our SCADA networks as well. The SCADA system is therefore well-defended." A SCADA security expert may say, of the very same network, "This is the most secure design possible given the business and technical requirements for the SCADA system, and so we have no choice but to accept all risks remaining in the design. The risks are by definition acceptable then, since we just accepted them, didn't we? Since only acceptable risks remain in the design, the defensive posture rates as 'good'."

Experts disagree as to the strength of defensive postures, and often disagree wildly.

The concept of "threat" in these qualitative assessments is just as nebulous. Threat in the context of a deliberate cyber-attack is widely regarded as a combination of our enemies' capabilities and intent, or motives [42], [43]. Our enemies' capabilities have been proven repeatedly. Even hacktivists routinely compromise networks protected by IT-style security programs.

If our SCADA systems have not been sabotaged recently, then this can be due to only one reason. Since threat is defined as capabilities coupled with intent, and the capabilities to sabotage us exist, then lack of recent sabotage means that our enemies currently have little motive to carry out such attacks.

What qualitative rank then, should we assign to our enemies' motives? A low number, because looking backward we see no recent targeted cyber-sabotage attacks on our organization's SCADA systems? A medium number, because today, we see the beginning of a trend in terms of organized crime using targeted attack techniques to seed ransomware? Or a large number, because we know there are motives for sophisticated attacks, ranging from stock market manipulation to industrial sabotage, and because we suspect that cleverly-disguised attacks might already be happening that we have not yet discovered?

In practice, industrial facilities in the Middle East, in Ukraine, and around the South China Sea assess their enemies' motives for cyber sabotage as "very high." Similar facilities in Western Europe generally assess their enemies' motives as "very low." This is true even when assessing the motives of exactly the same threat actors, against SCADA systems in the very same enterprise. One of these assessments is clearly incorrect.

In practice, the number we attribute to motive can change in a heartbeat, literally. All it takes is a single suspicious explosion in a facility we regard as similar, in some sense, to our own industrial site.

Our enemies' motives can change in a heartbeat as well. The erasure of 30,000 hard disks at Saudi Aramco was not the result of some technical breakthrough in attack capabilities. The attack was the result of shifting motives, and a decision to apply widely-understood cyber-espionage attack capabilities to the task of cyber sabotage.

Capabilities evolve much more slowly than motives. Prudent risk management should be based on proven attack capabilities, not perceived motives-of-the-moment.

Attack Modelling

Senior business decision-makers should not be called upon to make decisions based on fictional probabilities or hopelessly subjective qualitative metrics. A better way to make business decisions is starting to be called "attack modelling" [44]. Attack modelling communicates risks in terms of representative attack examples. Attack modelling is a new approach, but anecdotal evidence for this approach is growing.

For example, at a recent middle-eastern SCADA security conference, an employee of a major security consulting firm told a story. His firm had been contracted to produce a security assessment for a major refinery in the area. The firm was to produce the assessment, make recommendations for improving security, and provide cost estimates. The consulting firm was cautioned though, not to "get their hopes up." The owners of the refinery were paying for the assessment as part of a due diligence process. They felt that their security was already sufficient, and so no proposal for significant improvement was likely to be accepted.

Towards the end of the engagement, the employee met with the board of directors for the firm operating the refinery, to present interim findings. Part of the assessment was a penetration test, and the verbal report described how the firm's tester had broken into the SCADA network from the open Internet, and demonstrated an ability to see and manipulate the SCADA HMI software.

The consulting firm's preliminary funding proposal for an improved security system was accepted on the spot. "Fix this," the consultant was told. "We don't *ever* want this to happen again." While the average board member may understand fictional attack probabilities and subjective qualitative assessments very poorly, they seem to have a much finer appreciation of attack scenarios.

A fine point of interpretation on this example though – penetration tests are useful for shaking loose funding for improved security. Successful penetrations are dramatic proof of vulnerability. Penetration tests are a horrible security assessment technique, however. Penetration testers find only one way into a vulnerable system, not all of the ways in. If the consequence of a successful penetration is a "Band-Aid" solution applied to eliminate only the single attack vector the tester exploited, the resulting SCADA system is at best very marginally more secure than before the fix.

In another example, which illustrates this point, a SCADA security manager at a recent security symposium explained how his large oil company had successfully implemented a SCADA security program. This is a noteworthy accomplishment for a large organization. A large number of diverse sites, stakeholders, interests, approaches to automation and approaches to security make any comprehensive SCADA security program very difficult to implement.

The manager explained that his team had recruited a large number of third-party penetration testers to carry out "white box" analyses of a number of representative sites' security and SCADA systems. The testers' goal was to enumerate as many kinds of attacks on high-consequence systems as possible, within their budgets and scope of investigation. The SCADA security team reviewed the resulting large number of attack descriptions with process engineers. The review considered physical safety systems, digital safety systems, equipment protection systems, and other elements of the industrial design that might prevent serious consequences if any of the described cyber-attacks should occur. The review also collapsed multiple descriptions of very similar types of attacks into representative classes and examples.

The manager explained that the result was some twenty-two kinds of attacks that the combined attack / security / engineering team felt posed an unacceptable risk of causing serious consequences. For each attack, the team could explain how the attack defeated existing security mechanisms and other protections. The team then evaluated additional security measures and technologies against these attacks, seeking to identify a small set of measures to deploy universally, whose effects would be substantial mitigation of these attack risks. Part of the evaluation, of course, was a proposed budget to implement the measures.

When it came time to justify these measures to senior business decision-makers and other stake-holders in the organization, the team had only to lead the stake-holders through the example attack scenarios.

The lessons here are straightforward:

1) Focus on high-consequence attacks. For example, Langner's RIPE methodology starts with high-consequence "industrial incidents" [45]. The technique works backwards to understand what physical components are involved in such incidents, what computers control these physical components, and what paths for information flow exist to reach those computers and compromise them. Leave low-consequence attacks for traditional, backwards-looking, probabilities-based risk assessments.

2) Engage all of the specialists needed to evaluate such attacks. This generally includes attack specialists, cyber and physical defensive specialists, industrial process engineers, control systems engineers, safety specialists and equipment protection specialists. All of this expertise is critical to evaluating the credibility of high-consequence attack scenarios.

3) Enumerate a large set of attack scenarios with serious consequences. Then collapse similar attacks into categories, until a representative set of attack categories remains. Practitioners are starting to report good results using "bow-tie analysis" in this step [46]. Bow-tie analysis is a concept from safety system analysis that connects threats, consequences, and consequence-reduction mitigations with residual risks. A chain of "bow ties" illustrates a path from a normal state to a serious failure state.

4) Propose and cost security measures able to defeat each class of attacks reliably.

5) Present a cross-section of these examples of attack classes to senior decision-makers and other stakeholders. Ask them to rank the attacks as to which represent risks the organization should take steps to mitigate, transfer, or accept.

Revisiting Expert Advice

With this methodology in mind, it is possible to revisit the advice presented by the SCADA security panel summarized at the beginning of this chapter.

a) "Security is pure cost."

If this is true of SCADA security, then it is true of every form of risk mitigation or transferal. The benefit to spending money on SCADA security is reduced risk. Some costs, pure or otherwise, must be paid. This is something every business person understands.

b) "There has to be an ROI for every one of our security investments, so we use a risk-based approach."

Return on investment is generally measured in dollars. Saying there must be an ROI for every security investment means the only investments the organization will consider are those that can be quantified in dollars. The only SCADA security risks that can be quantified are backwards-looking, LIHF risks. Doing nothing at all about HILF risks is a bad idea for most organizations.

c) "Cyber risk calculations can't be quantitative, so we use a qualitative approach. This makes ROI calculations impossible."

The problem with a qualitative approach is the subjectivity of qualitative scores, and the difficulty of communicating the results of the risk assessment to business decision-makers. Communicating risk as abstract, subjective scores generally does not yield useful business decisions. Summarizing and communicating risk as representative attacks and consequences is still communicating risk qualitatively, but with less of the subjective baggage that comes with the standard abstract scoring approach.

d) "It's simpler than that – just never be the highest-ranked person to know about a risk. Always make your boss sign off on it."

On the surface, this advice might seem cynical and self-serving, but the comment has some merit. The highest levels of management are the ones who should be aware of the kinds of risks the business is undertaking, and should be involved to some degree in deciding how to address those risks.

e) "It all depends on the risk appetite of your board and executive."

This is very true. Different organizations have different risk appetites. Start-ups, for example, with no income but what comes from seed investors, routinely take comparatively much larger business risks than do public utilities which enjoy local monopolies for some product or service.

In all cases though, it is vital that we be able to explain SCADA security risks and consequences to business decision-makers in a manner that they understand. There is no other way those decision-makers can confidently compare risks and dispositions to what they believe should be the organization's appetite for risk.

Questions For Boards To Ask Executives

Board members should be alarmed when they hear their CIO say things that betray either a complete lack of SCADA security knowledge, or an attitude that implies that board members are unable to understand SCADA risk decisions. Tell-tale phrases include:

- "Nothing can get into our SCADA systems." Nothing is secure.
- "We have secured our SCADA systems to an appropriate degree," and later on "Penetration tests on our live systems are too dangerous." Both of these cannot be true of the same system. After all, our enemies seek to penetrate our live systems. Generally speaking, our enemies have greater talent and resources available to them than we are able to purchase. Saying that our own testers represent an unacceptable risk is an admission that our enemies represent such a risk as well.
- "Our control systems are too complex / diverse / redundant to hack." The complexity/diversity/redundancy argument is an old one, and incorrect. Nothing is secure. Everything can be hacked. None of these attributes saved the Ukrainian power-distribution companies, or the German steel mill, did they?

- "No high-impact consequences are possible, because of the design of our safety/protection systems." This is a harder one. It is sometimes possible to design physical safety systems that reliably prevent the most serious consequences, but it is difficult for senior managers to determine that this has been done. In addition, industrial facility downtime can be very costly, even if there are no injuries and there is no damaged equipment.

For example, consider the Texas City Refinery explosion again. The refinery was protected by an extensive system of physical safety devices. The explosion was caused by the plant operator misoperating the SCADA system's HMI in the face of the failure of a single tank-level sensor. Both of these conditions could be simulated by malware or a remote attacker in a worst-case cyber assault. The robustness of the site's physical safety systems had evidently never been evaluated against the combination of circumstances that caused the explosion.

Stating "our safety systems will save us" without compelling evidence, say in the form of an extensive investigation of possible failures and regular reviews thereof, is much more likely to be wishful thinking than hard, cold analysis. Most safety systems have never been evaluated for cyber risk, where multiple components can be forced to fail simultaneously, rather than at random. Worse, even when such cyber / safety risk evaluations are carried out, they are most often carried out with highly subjective, qualitative data.

More generally, when assured that a suitable SCADA security risk management system is in place and working, board members really should ask for the next level of detail. Absolutely every such program must enumerate and classify possible high-consequence attacks. Every such program must evaluate those potential attacks against defensive postures. Any hint the board gets that this has not in fact been done recently should be cause for alarm.

Questions board members should consider asking, when assured that SCADA security risks have been addressed:

"What kind of SCADA security attack scenarios has the risk management program considered?" There are an infinite number of possible attacks. Saying "all attacks have been considered" is clearly nonsense.

"What is the simplest, high-consequence attack scenario that our defenses do not defeat with a high degree of confidence?" An answer such as "there are none such" is incorrect. For example, consider again an attack where each and every one of the company's employees and contractors has been bribed by our enemies. There is always a simplest attack that we do not defeat with a high degree of confidence. The CIO really should know some examples of attacks and consequences the SCADA security risk management team decided to accept.

"What is the worst-case consequence of that simplest attack scenario?" If the only answer we receive is "the plant shuts down," probe deeper. For most physical processes, there are much more serious consequences possible.

"What is an example of a sophisticated, high-consequence attack scenario that our defenses do defeat with a high degree of confidence?" Then ask "For this scenario, what defensive capabilities should reassure us that the attack scenario will be defeated reliably?"

Listen carefully to the explanation for this last question. How much of the explanation assumes "unhackable" security software or other software? All software can be hacked. How much of the defensive posture has to do with detection and incident response, rather than outright prevention of compromise? Turbines and human lives cannot be "restored from backup" the way IT systems can. How much of the defensive posture is predicated on catching the intrusion in the IT network, before the attackers have opportunity to penetrate into the SCADA network? IT networks are porous by design, and we should assume they are constantly compromised. SCADA defenses should not rely on the impenetrability of the essentially un-defendable IT network.

If a board hears unacceptable answers to these questions, it is a sign that the organization is exposed unacceptably to SCADA security risks. Persuading a CEO of this can be difficult though – when the board and the CIO disagree about a technical matter, who should the CEO believe?

This is a serious problem. It is possible to describe technical solutions to technical SCADA security problems in a book such as this one, but persuading the world's cyber-security experts that their IT-centric view of SCADA systems has been wrong for the last 15 years is much more difficult.

A possible solution might be to propose bringing in a third party to carry out a penetration test of the live SCADA system, while the plant is in full production. An answer from the CIO of "that's too dangerous" might serve to persuade the CEO that something is amiss. Again, our enemies generally have better access to attack talent than we are able to purchase ourselves. An admission that our own testers represent an unacceptable risk to operations is an admission that our enemies attackers do as well.

Summary

Quantitative risk assessments do not apply to HILF events, because we have no probabilities we can assign to these events reliably, and we should not ask business decision-makers to make decisions based on fictional probabilities. Qualitative risk assessments are notoriously subjective, especially when it comes to evaluating how well-protected a SCADA network is.

Business decision-makers generally understand attack scenarios and consequences better than subjective, qualitative risk scores. Communicating risk in terms of example attacks with high consequences leads to more effective decision-making. There are rules of thumb and lines of questioning that board members can use to determine when information presented to them by security executives is suspect.

Recommended Reading

Robust Control System Networks, 2012, by Ralph Langner

Cyber-risk, Standards and Best Practices, by Paul Feldman and Dan Hill, Electricity Policy, 2015

Chapter 10 – "Secure" Remote Access

With a description of the SCADA security problem and its solution behind us, we consider some sore spots that are points of vigorous disagreement in the SCADA security community in light of the preventive approach to SCADA security.

Specifically, a unidirectionally-protected cyber perimeter makes modern, sophisticated remote control attacks physically impossible. This is a very good thing. This prevents any possibility that our enemies can reprogram our SCADA systems while sipping coffee in their basements on another continent. However, preventing remote access also means preventing us, ourselves, from reprogramming and repairing our own SCADA systems while sipping coffee in our hotel rooms after the conference we are attending, or during the vacation we are trying to enjoy. Remote access and remote control make life easier for all of us as well as for our enemies. Can we not "have our cake and eat it too?"

Looking deeper, the technical term we are discussing here is "interactive remote access." Interactive remote access provides the ability to reach into our SCADA network from distant locations, and interact with that network as if we were local. Remote Desktop, Citrix, SSH and even some kinds of web meeting software are all interactive remote access tools. These tools let us type commands into distant SCADA computers as if we were local. These tools frequently have the ability to show us the screens on those distant computers, and let us move the mouse as well. And yes, these capabilities are precisely the features built into modern attack tools as well as the remote access tools we use ourselves.

Is there no way to do this "securely?" After all, there are countless documents available explaining how to set up "secure remote access" [47], [48], [49], [50]. Recall though, the first law of cybersecurity: nothing is secure. Everyone using "secure" as an adjective, as in "secure remote access," is either selling something, or has just bought something.

Looking around, it certainly seems that a lot of people are selling remote access, and not just security technology vendors. NERC for example, published "Guidance for Secure Interactive Remote Access" in 2011 [47]. Why? Because the vast majority of the electric utilities that are members of NERC want remote access. They are hoping that NERC's regulator – the Federal Energy Regulatory Commission (FERC) – and other regulatory authorities will "buy" the "secure remote access" that NERC is selling.

"But wait, wait!" cry the IT guys at the back of the room. "We have encryption! We have firewalls! We have two-factor authentication! We have jump hosts! And our jump hosts are right up to date with the latest antivirus signatures, security updates and intrusion detection agents! We are right up to date with the very latest IT best practices! Surely this makes us secure?"

We remind the IT guys that nothing is secure.

Attacking "Secure" Remote Access

To understand these "secure remote access" systems, consider Figure (7). A laptop in some hotel room connects through the hotel's firewall to the Internet. It reaches through the Internet with an encrypted Virtual Private Network (VPN) connection. The connection is encrypted, so it must be "secure." The VPN connects the laptop to a host running Remote Desktop or some other remote access tool. This host is called an "intermediate host" or a "jump host" because the host is not part of the SCADA network. Instead, the host is a "jumping off point" that provides us with access to the protected SCADA network. The jump host has access to SCADA hosts through a firewall. A process engineer can be sipping coffee in the hotel room, logged into the jump host, and reaching through the jump host into the SCADA network, reprogramming parts of the network.

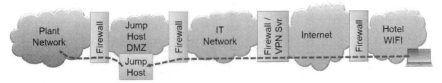

Figure (7): "Secure" Interactive Remote Access

How do our enemies breach this "secure remote access?"

Our enemies break into this "secure" system using a spear-phishing attack to steal a password and simply log in. Often the VPN will have the same password as the jump host – that was the "single sign-on" feature we paid so much for. The VPN buys no protection here – the VPN happily encrypts attacks as thoroughly as it encrypts legitimate traffic.

The IT guys are correct in asserting that two-factor authentication helps somewhat. Two-factor is when we need at least two "things" to log in – generally a password and something else, such as an RSA key fob, a fingerprint, or sometimes just a secret encryption key hidden in the laptop's hardware. Breaking two-factor authentication is easier or harder, depending on the type of the authentication. Finger-print readers continue to be broken, one after the other. Encryption keys can sometimes be stolen. If the key is stored in a Trusted Platform Module (TPM) the key is harder to steal, but a bit of malware on the laptop can do the job. The malware can use the hidden key and the TPM hardware to reach into a critical network in the same way that legitimate software on that laptop uses the laptop's hardware.

An attack that defeats even two-factor systems is malware on the laptop that waits until the remote engineer logs in. The engineer logs in with all the two-factoring, TPM, finger-printing, iris-scanning and other identification testing that may be necessary. The malware then takes over the interactive session, hiding the window showing the screen of the remote computer, and displaying an error dialog to distract the engineer – perhaps something saying, "Remote Desktop has stopped responding. Click here to check for a solution."

A little bit of programming is all that is needed to carry out this attack. Malware developers can test their new code against all existing antivirus systems, to be doubly sure none of them detect the malware. The developers just wrote the malware though, so it is most likely that none of the AV systems will have any signatures for it in the first place.

How Can This Be?

Given these vulnerabilities, why do IT people configure remote access to IT networks in the first place? It is because, as we saw in Chapter 4, IT networks are in a state of more or less constant compromise, with incident response teams constantly fighting the fight. Most of the malware used to compromise IT networks has interactive remote control capabilities. In this environment, another few attacks per year that yield remote control to our attackers do not represent a significant increase in overall risk. Such attacks add up to only another few machines for the incident response team to clean out.

Moreover, when compromise occurs on IT networks, most IT teams see the consequences as manageable. Most IT intrusions are attempts to steal data. Intrusion detection systems and data-exfiltration-prevention systems do a reasonable job of detecting intrusions before very much data has been stolen. When the compromised computers are identified, incident response teams can erase them and restore them from backup.

With control systems, again, we cannot restore damaged turbines or human lives "from backups." Unlike IT security experts, SCADA security practitioners generally see even the briefest deliberate compromise or misoperation of control system components as an unacceptable risk.

Unidirectional Remote Screen View

Counter-intuitively, most of the benefits of remote access systems are in fact available to thoroughly-protected SCADA systems, provided the right technology platforms and policies are deployed.

Unidirectional remote screen view (RSV) is one technology that can help. This technology is used routinely to provide one type of remote access to unidirectionally-protected networks. RSV is used most commonly by "outsider" third parties, third parties who have not been through an organization's personnel background checks, security training programs, or security awareness programs.

The classic example is turbine monitoring vendors. Steam, gas and water turbines are all rotating equipment, under enormous physical stress. Vibration is the enemy of all rotating equipment, and many turbine vendors will not provide a warranty or support contract for a turbine unless those vendors can monitor the turbine constantly for vibration anomalies, and have remote access to the turbine control system from time to time to correct those anomalies before they turn into catastrophic failures.

Unidirectional gateways are deployed routinely for the monitoring function, replicating turbine control-system components to another network for monitoring by the turbine vendors. The vendors' monitoring technology generally has no idea it is working with a replica, since the unidirectional replica is a faithful and accurate copy of the turbine control components. However, when a vibration or other problem is detected, the gateways mean the turbine vendors have no way to log into the turbine control system to alter that system to correct the problem.

Instead, the turbine vendor picks up the phone and calls the site to schedule maintenance activity. When the appointed time arrives, someone at the site calls the turbine vendor and sits down at the turbine control workstation. The person at the site activates the remote screen view client on the workstation.

The RSV client starts taking pictures of the screen, and sends those pictures through the unidirectional hardware to an external web server. The vendor logs into that web server with VPNs and passwords and any other security the IT team has set up. Logged in, the vendor can see the screen of the protected workstation, but of course can move her mouse and type on the keyboard as much as she wishes, no signal can return through the unidirectional gateway into the protected network.

Instead, the vendor gives instructions over the phone to the person at the site. "Bring up the vibration diagnostics system please. No, no. That's system diagnostics. Two further down. There you go – that's the vibration diagnostics."

The vendor can see the protected workstation's screen, can see the mouse moving, and can give second-by-second advice to the person at the site as to how to correct the problem according to the vendor's procedures.

The vendor perceives the process as supervising site personnel to ensure that a complex problem is corrected "properly." The site engineer sees the process as supervising the vendor, and keeps notes or a log as to what the vendor has done to the site's turbine.

Both perspectives are legitimate.

Emergency Bypass

Remote screen view works well when there is a qualified, authorized individual at the industrial site to interact with remote support personnel. This may not be the case in a reliability emergency, or worse, in a safety emergency. In such emergencies, security measures had better not impair emergency response. The top priorities for deploying strong cyber-security protections at a site are protecting the safety and the reliability of the industrial process, which means security systems are worthless if they ever materially impair safety and reliability.

Emergency bypass technology can be used to support emergency response. An emergency bypass unit is generally deployed in parallel with unidirectional gateway security mechanisms, as illustrated in Figure (8). In its normal state, the bypass hardware blocks all communications through the unit. The bypass unit is activated manually, for example by someone at the site physically pushing a button on the unit, turning a key, or entering a numeric code. When the bypass hardware is activated, it enables a conventional two-way network connection past the unidirectional gateway.

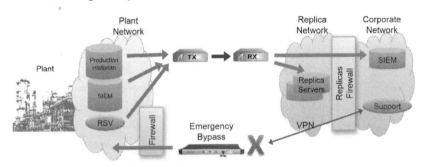

Figure (8): Emergency bypass

This network connection, as illustrated in the Figure, generally leads to a conventional VPN/jump host, with two-factor authentication, and a variety of anti-malware, security update, intrusion detection and other conventional remote access security measures. In short, for as long as the emergency bypass unit is engaged, conventional interactive remote access is enabled to the SCADA network. This allows remote responders to log in and work to address the SCADA system's emergency.

This means that the SCADA system is exposed to remote access threats for the duration of the emergency, and is immune from such threats otherwise. Even if an attacker is able to use the opportunity of an emergency at the site to plant modern remote-control malware at the site through an emergency responder's remote access session, this attacker can operate the malware only while the remote bypass unit is engaged. This slows down remote attacks by orders of magnitude, greatly increasing the likelihood that the attack can be discovered and thwarted before lasting damage is done.

Automated Remote Maintenance

WAN-based SCADA systems, such as those controlling pipelines and electric grids, interact routinely with equipment at hundreds or thousands of small, distant, unstaffed sites. Many of these sites require occasional routine maintenance and emergency trouble-shooting, but there is no person at the site to activate remote screen view or emergency bypass systems. At these sites, SCADA owners and operators deploy inbound/outbound gateways with maintenance connectors enabled.

The inbound and outbound gateways at each site generally deal with maintenance issues, as well as with whatever SCADA protocol is used by equipment at the site. This latter is for example, commonly one of Modbus, DNP3, IEC 60870-5-104, or IEC 61850. The gateways replicate the central SCADA system's protocol server into the distant site, and replicate the site's devices out to the SCADA WAN, where the central protocol server can see the replicas. This enables the central SCADA system to gather information about physical industrial equipment at the site from the outbound replica, and to send any commands to the inbound replica that may be needed to control that physical equipment.

The maintenance connector deals with unusual conditions. If equipment at the site has failed outright, and must be replaced, there is generally no choice but to dispatch a crew to the site to replace the offending components. When the problem at the site is a software problem though, as it is in a large fraction of cases, remote repairs are often possible without the costly step of dispatching a crew to the site. In addition, if some degree of remote diagnostics is possible, it is often possible to diagnose a physical problem through a maintenance connector with a high degree of confidence, and thus ensure that personnel sent to repair the site have the necessary spare parts and training.

The maintenance connector takes advantage of the fact that these remote sites are generally small, comparatively simple, and the most common maintenance problems are well-understood. The connector is controlled by a central application, such as a web server, that displays information to technicians and allows technicians to issue requests to the site.

For example, consider a case where a central management team sees an alarm in the SCADA system saying that a replica device on the SCADA WAN at an electric substation is responding more and more slowly to

SCADA requests as time goes by. A maintenance technician at the central site logs into the central maintenance application, selects "Slow Response Alarm" from a top-level menu of symptoms, and enters the name of the affected substation.

In this example, the central application sends the number "27" to the maintenance connector of the inbound gateway at the substation. The maintenance connector communicates that number to the substation side of the inbound unidirectional gateway. The substation side does some sanity checks, such as checking that a maintenance scenario numbered "27" exists. If the checks pass, the maintenance connector activates maintenance script number 27. A maintenance script is a sequence of commands that query site equipment to gather additional diagnostic details, or modify substation equipment in preprogrammed and approved ways. In this example, script "27" contains commands that log into every piece of equipment at the site and gather CPU usage, memory usage, and communications channel usage from all of that equipment, depositing the results in a file server that the outbound gateway replicates back to the central site.

At the central site, the maintenance application shows the results to the technician, who observes that serial device number 4 is sending an unusually large amount of information to the substation automation controller, and this is likely what is impairing the responsiveness of that controller. The technician presses another button, which sends the command "43" to the maintenance controller. Maintenance script "43" logs into the automation controller, enables serial DNP3 packet tracing on serial device number 4 for 30 seconds, and sends the packet trace file to the substation's file server.

The technician examines the packet trace and sees that it consists almost entirely of "report by exception" messages as a single value flips between two states. The technician scans through notes left in this part of the maintenance application by other technicians over time, and sees that this condition is usually the result of the failure of a particular electrical sensor at the substation. Accordingly, the technician logs a request in the maintenance system to dispatch a crew to the site, a crew equipped with a suitable replacement sensor.

In short, the maintenance connector provides for a set of preprogrammed maintenance activities for distant, unstaffed sites, encoded in known maintenance "actions" or "scripts." These preprogrammed actions were developed by SCADA engineers over time, and deployed to the sites as part of the unidirectional gateway deployments at the sites.

The maintenance connector not only serves to enable remote maintenance of distant sites, but serves to reduce errors and omissions as well. Much of the equipment at these distant sites has few security features – any technician logging into the equipment has the ability to do just about anything to the equipment, such as changing configurations, activating detailed diagnostic features, rebooting the device, changing the software in the device, and sometimes even erasing hard drives or otherwise rendering the device permanently inoperable.

A maintenance connector not only enables remote maintenance of unidirectionally-protected sites, it permits only those remote actions that SCADA engineers have deemed acceptable. The maintenance connector not only makes it much more difficult for attackers to execute damaging commands at a remote site, the connector makes it much more difficult for legitimate users to make mistakes that cause lasting damage to the site as well.

Operations WAN

In many organizations, the engineering function has been centralized – even large industrial sites may have no engineers at the sites any more, only technicians. A central engineering team means engineers have easier access to each other, for training, mentoring and consultation. In a central engineering function, specialization is possible, optimizations and significant cost savings can be found, and certain kinds of career growth are available that simply do not exist in smaller engineering groups at widely-distributed sites.

What this means security-wise though, is that a large fraction of the central team must connect remotely to complex equipment in distant industrial sites essentially all day long. The changes engineers make are not the kind that can be automated, the way we automate the changes technicians make to small, distant and unstaffed sites. RSV, emergency bypass units and remote maintenance solutions do not meet the needs of these engineering teams.

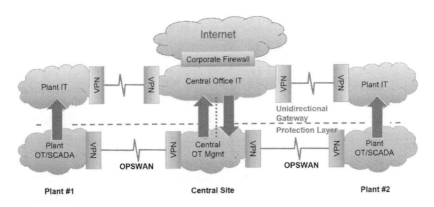

Figure (9) An Operations WAN

Instead, these teams tend to deploy an operations WAN (OPSWAN) as illustrated in Figure (9). An OPSWAN is a wide-area network that connects one or more control system or "operations" networks to a central site. Ideally, dedicated networking infrastructure is used to create the OPSWAN, but this is not always possible. Always though, VPN products are used to protect communications across all WAN connections, and often multiple layers of VPN products to reduce the possibility that a single vulnerability in such a product can lead to network compromise.

Cyber-security-wise, this means that all of the control systems at the sites on the OPSWAN as well as at the central site become one security zone. This means that all of these sites must be protected to the level of the most sensitive site on the WAN.

In particular, it means that none of this equipment, not even the engineering workstations at the central site, can be permitted to exchange messages, directly or indirectly, with the Internet. We saw earlier how an Internet-exposed remote-access laptop could be compromised, and used to misoperate industrial equipment. If any machine at all on the OPSWAN can exchange messages with the Internet, that machine can be compromised and used to launch an attack on the rest of the OPSWAN.

This does not mean we deny electronic mail and Internet access to the central engineering team. Most often, it means that every member of the central team has two computers in her office. A (red) corporate workstation or laptop is able to do dangerous things, such as browsing the Internet and reading email. This computer is connected to the corporate IT network. A (blue) operations workstation is connected to one of the

102

OPSWAN networks at the central site, and is able to reach into and reprogram all of the equipment at all of the sites on that network.

The only connection between any sub-network on the OPSWAN and corporate networks or vendor networks is via unidirectional-gateway or related technologies. These may be deployed at each site, or there may be one larger deployment at the central site, subject to expert central oversight. Either way, messages from the Internet are never routed into any part of the OPSWAN.

Variations on this theme are possible as well. A single, very large OPSWAN becomes increasingly dangerous as the number of sites, pieces of equipment and people on that OPSWAN increases. Deploying several smaller OPSWANs limits consequences if one network somehow becomes compromised, and reduces the benefits of a central engineering team only marginally. When multiple OPSWANs are deployed to the same central site, engineering workstations at the central site can only be connected to one OPSWAN, and cannot be "switched" at all routinely between OPSWANs. To reconnect a central engineering workstation to a different OPSWAN is equivalent to physically carrying that workstation past security at a new site and plugging it into the control network at that site. This is an action that nobody would carry out without serious scrutiny, because the workstation's hard drive contains countless files and information, all of which could be an attack.

There are physical security implications for this OPSWAN concept as well. Again, because all sites on one OPSWAN have access to all of the other sites via the central engineering extension of the OPSWAN, any compromise of one site is at risk of propagating to other sites. This means that cyber and physical security precautions for all of the sites on the WAN, including the central engineering site must be as stringent as the most stringent such precautions at the most sensitive site on the WAN.

Our enemies will always attack our weakest links. Poorly-secured sites must not be able to reach our most sensitive, most dangerous, or most important sites through the OPSWAN, or by pivoting through hosts at the central site.

Reprogramming SCADA Systems From Our Cell Phones

Regulatory authorities are starting to recognize the dangers of conventional "secure" remote access. The 2010 American and 2015

Canadian nuclear generator regulations forbid software-based remote access to nuclear reactor control systems [23], [24]. The 2014 French ANSSI regulations go further, strongly discouraging remote access to their "Class 2" networks, which include most critical infrastructures, and strictly forbidding remote access to their "Class 3" networks, which include most digital safety systems [25]. Disciplined remote access to unidirectionally-protected networks is possible in terms of remote screen view, emergency bypass units, and central engineering OPSWANs.

What does this mean for our ability to reprogram our own SCADA systems while sitting in a basement on another continent, sipping coffee? On a panel at a recent cyber security conference, a number of leading SCADA security authorities were discussing the dangers of interactive remote access in the context of the North American electric sector's NERC CIP standards. In the question period, there was a question from the floor. The question was more or less, "It's easy for you to sit there and talk about the dangers of remote access, but we live in the real world. What are we supposed to do when there is a *compelling business need* for remote access? This happens. What then?"

The answer from a panel member was "If you have a *compelling business need* to control a 2 gigawatt power plant from your cell phone while you're stopped at a traffic light, NERC CIP can't help you. Nobody can. You're on your own with that. Let us know how that works for you."

Summary

Anyone talking about "secure remote access" is either selling something, or has been sold something. What IT teams call "secure remote access" is easily defeated. This risk appears to be acceptable for IT networks because those networks are assumed to be constantly compromised already.

Unidirectional remote screen view can provide remote access to staffed sites, and requires active cooperation from an insider at the SCADA site. OPSWANs can provide continuous, central access to SCADA systems, but cyber and physical security precautions at all sites on the OPSWAN must be equivalent to the protections mandated for the most sensitive site on that WAN. Remote screen view and an OPSWAN can be combined to permit personnel at the central site to help remote support personnel gain access to distant sites, even distant unstaffed sites. Emergency bypass units can be used to relax cyber-perimeter security measures for the duration of declared safety or reliability emergencies, and again require the active cooperation of an individual at the SCADA site.

All this means that most of the benefits of remote access are available to thoroughly-protected SCADA systems, without incurring the risks that always accompany IT-class "secure" remote access systems.

Recommended Reading

Alert IR-ALERT-H-16-056-01 Cyber-Attack Against Ukrainian Critical Infrastructure, 2016, U.S. Department of Homeland Security Industrial Control Systems Computer Emergency Response Team

"How long do you want these messages to remain secret?
... I want them to remain secret for as long as men
are capable of evil."

-- *Neal Stephenson, Cryptonomicon, 1999*

Chapter 11 – Encryption

A second point of widespread disagreement in the SCADA security community may not be evident to outsiders. Encryption is used nearly universally on IT networks, and is used as well when SCADA communications pass across the Internet, to prevent unauthorized viewing or tampering. Without encryption, every time we logged in from a Wi-Fi hotspot, or provided our credit card numbers online, we would be at serious risk of having our login credentials and account numbers stolen.

Since encryption is used almost universally on IT networks, many security experts maintain that the same should be true on SCADA networks, even though data theft is generally a low priority on such networks. Many SCADA practitioners and even some SCADA security experts disagree. Few go on record expressing such disagreement though, since they can be ridiculed if they do [51].

Authentication

Technically, the debate is not supposed to be about encryption – modern encryption protocols provide many elements, including mechanisms for encryption key exchange, hiding the contents of messages, and ensuring that the contents of messages came from an authentic sender. So more precisely, many experts maintain that strong, cryptographic authentication techniques should be used for important SCADA communications, since preventing unauthorized control should be the focus of security for most SCADA networks, rather than preventing data theft.

However, since cryptographic authentication is built into most encryption technologies, simply using these technologies to encrypt communications is often the easiest way to provide message authentication. While it is possible to use cryptographic authentication codes in un-encrypted messages, this combination of technologies is used very little on IT networks. Thus, many SCADA system designers are reluctant to use authentication without encryption, because little-used combinations of even the most popular technologies tend to be less than reliable, and tend to be low priorities for repair by the vendors maintaining those technologies.

Insecure By Design

The encryption debate is poorly documented. Most published advice and best-practices encourage us to use encryption and authentication as widely as possible in our SCADA systems. For example, Digital Bond's long-standing "insecure by design" campaign is critical of many SCADA vendors [52]. The vendors are criticized for building insecure modes of operation into their products. Why would an attacker bother finding a vulnerability in the software of an industrial device, if that attacker can simply tell the device to load the attacker's own firmware, or send commands to the device to manipulate the physical world, and have the device carry out those commands without question?

While the "insecure by design" campaign does not explicitly call out encryption as the solution to the problem, most of the complaints against vendors are about unauthorized remote operations. Strong cryptographic authorization codes, and associated software changes, would generally address these complaints.

Cryptographic authentication is designed to prevent attacks where unauthorized third parties impersonate legitimate systems and so misoperate physical equipment. For example, say there is a file server on a SCADA network that is used to make daily back-up copies of important files. If an attacker breaks into this server, the compromised server can be made to send commands to whatever device the attacker wants. Without strong authentication systems, the industrial devices receiving these commands simply carry them out. With authentication systems in place, in principle at least, such attacks should fail, because the devices have not been configured to regard the file server as authorized to send commands to the devices.

Limitations of Encryption/Authentication

Like all security technologies though, cryptographic authentication and related technologies have limitations. When attackers have compromised the real SCADA systems that legitimately send commands to equipment, authentication is no protection against attack. In these cases, an attacker can use the compromised SCADA computers to send control messages to industrial devices with full authentication, because these computers legitimately have access to all encryption keys and other information needed to produce authentic commands.

This is in addition to the standard vulnerabilities that come from software. Authentication mechanisms are software, and all software can be hacked. Such attacks do require a bit of research to find relevant software vulnerabilities, but it is generally possible to launch attacks at the software that receives authenticated commands. Once a device is compromised, it can be told to do whatever the attacker wishes, authentication codes or not.

Finally, authentication codes depend on cryptographic keys. Intercepting keys during distribution, compromising key repositories, or compromising certificate authorities that authenticate key exchanges are also ways to attack cryptographic authentication.

Debating Encryption

All that said, encryption and authentication technologies do provide a degree of protection from certain kinds of attacks. SCADA practitioners reluctant to deploy encryption and authentication technologies generally point out that most of the unprotected, unauthenticated and therefore vulnerable communications, take place deep within the physical and cyber security perimeters protecting SCADA systems. These practitioners argue that encryption provides few additional protections this deep into security perimeters, and introduces additional costs and risks.

The strongest encryption and authentication codes, for example, can consume significant computing resources. The computers closest to physical equipment are often low-power, environmentally-hardened equipment, which may not have the capacity for costly cryptographic calculations in addition to the real-time monitoring and control this equipment must carry out.

The most popular IT encryption systems can also introduce significant latencies and delays into certain kinds of communications, delays that may be unacceptable in real-time systems.

Practitioners who oppose encryption also point out that encryption makes third-party decoding and verification of messages more difficult. An inability to decode control and monitoring messages can impair some network intrusion-detection systems, as well as both normal and emergency debugging efforts.

Finally, practitioners also point out that best practices for management of cryptographic keys can impair reliability and safety. IT best practices demand that cryptographic keys expire and be replaced on a regular basis, and that expired keys be rejected by communications endpoints. This management discipline increases costs on SCADA systems, and increases opportunities for errors and omissions. A single missed, expired encryption key can impair safety or reliability so much that an entire site is subject to an unscheduled emergency shutdown.

Primary vs Secondary Protections

This said, practitioners and experts generally agree that encryption or authentication constitute primary protections when communicating across wide-area networks. WAN communications pass outside of any physical or cyber-security perimeter. These communications are therefore exposed to attack in ways that LAN communications are simply not exposed.

Where experts and practitioners disagree is in the realm of LAN-based communications with industrial devices deep inside of security perimeters. These disagreements have the flavor of a "religious" difference – no argument made by one side seems to move the other side in the least.

Looking at this "religious" difference in light of prevention-centric security practices suggests a simple resolution. In networks protected primarily by IT-style detection/response-centric security programs, encryption and authentication adds significant security value. In such systems, remote-control attacks into the most important parts of SCADA systems are likely to occur, because modern attacks routinely defeat IT-style primary protections, including security updates, anti-malware systems and intrusion detection/response programs.

If we assume that our enemies are able to take remote control of random computers on our industrial device networks, additional protections for those networks are needed. Encryption and authentication force attackers to take over specific, authorized command servers, whereas "insecure by design" equipment allows any compromised machine to send arbitrary commands throughout the entire industrial network. In these very vulnerable networks, encryption increases somewhat the difficulty for our attackers, and increases somewhat our hopes of detecting our attackers before damage is done.

In networks with strong security perimeters though, including at least one layer of unidirectional gateways and a strong security program controlling removable media and transient devices, this disagreement over encryption is less important. Modern, remote-control attacks on such networks are not possible, and introducing autonomous malware via removable media and transient devices is very difficult as well. Encryption is a secondary control on these networks, not a primary control as on IT-style networks.

This means it is entirely reasonable to control our investments in encryption and authentication. For example, we really should insist that our vendors provide strong authentication mechanisms for non-time-sensitive operations, such as loading new firmware, because strong authentication for such operations marginally improves security, without significantly impacting cost, safety or reliability. We should also deploy encryption and authentication everywhere, in even our deepest industrial network, any time that the cost and consequences of doing so are minimal.

However, when it comes to introducing new safety and reliability risks, we should be reluctant to encrypt or authenticate as comprehensively as is indicated on constantly-compromised IT networks. For example, if strong encryption is impractical on low-powered devices, deep within our best-protected SCADA networks, then weaker encryption should be deployed.

In another example, it is entirely reasonable to configure no key expiry dates at all on our most critical SCADA networks, deep behind prevention-centric protections [53]. Encryption without key expiry conveys most of the benefits of strong IT-style encryption and authentication systems, without impairing safety and reliability. Strict, IT-style encryption and IT-style key management do provide very small additional protections, but do so by introducing unacceptable risks.

The way forward for the debate seems clear. Anyone foolish enough to protect a reliability-critical or safety-critical SCADA system with only IT-style protections is well-advised to deploy encryption, authentication, intrusion detection and the whole panoply of IT security mechanisms. Such SCADA sites should also prepare to be compromised, start practicing their incident response plans, and recognize that there is a significant risk that they will not catch their intruders before the lights go out, or other physical consequences arise.

Summary

Message authentication codes are cryptographic assurance for message authenticity, and the simplest way to apply these protections to SCADA communications is by using standard message encryption techniques. Encryption is a primary preventive control for communications passing through a WAN. Encryption is a primary preventive control for all SCADA systems protected by only IT-class security measures, such as security updates, antivirus systems, and intrusion detection systems, but we have already established that such designs are unwise.

In a properly-protected SCADA network, encryption constitutes a secondary protective measure, addressing only residual risks. Anyone protecting SCADA networks with prevention-centric approaches should still deploy as much encryption as is practical.

Strict IT-style encryption or authentication schemes often introduce significant costs, safety risks and reliability risks. When encryption is a secondary protection, we can and should relax these IT requirements that introduce more risk than they mitigate. Often it is possible to relax strict IT-style encryption requirements to produce an encryption system that adds a marginal degree of security value, without impairing safety and reliability.

Recommended Reading

Practical Cryptography, 2003, by Niels Ferguson and Bruce Schneier

"The big, unanswered question with the Internet of Things
is not 'is my private data secure?'
but rather 'are these devices
that control parts of my physical world safe?'"

-- *Lior Frenkel,*
The Internet of Things – Is It Safe?
Remote Site & Equipment Management, 2014

Chapter 12 – The Industrial Internet of Things

The IT guys at the back of the room are restless. The perimeter-focused, prevention-centric security strategy sounds right, but is at odds with the bright perimeter-less future we hear IT security gurus predicting. In this chapter, we apply the prevention-centric security approach to the bright, cloud-centric future of SCADA systems: the Industrial Internet of Things (IIoT). We need to understand how we can reap the benefits of the IIoT, without introducing deadly safety risks and debilitating reliability risks.

The IIoT is the industrial application of the Internet of Things (IoT) [54]. The IoT is small computers connected to the physical world, communicating with each other and with distant "cloud" computer systems across the Internet.

For an example of the IoT, consider a kitchen stovetop. It is already possible to buy such appliances with touch-screen controls. In these stovetops, the computer behind the touch screen is controlling whether the stove's burners are turned on or not. The touch-screen computer is also connected to a home automation center over a wireless network, and the home automation center is connected to some Internet cloud. Owners of modern stoves can now connect to the cloud from their cell phones and see how much electric power their stoves are using. Isn't this clever?

But – all software can be hacked, and every message can be an attack. The home automation network is also connected to the TV, which can browse the Internet. Imagine that we download a virus to the TV. The TV virus reaches out and takes over the home automation center. The compromised home automation center sends encrypted, authenticated, wireless attack messages to the stove, compromising the touch-screen computer using a previously-unknown software vulnerability. The compromised stove turns all of the burners on to maximum, at 2:00 AM.

This same virus does exactly the same thing to one hundred thousand other homes on Christmas Eve. In five thousand of those homes, something was left on the burners, catching fire. One thousand homes burn to the ground. One hundred people die. Some terrorist group claims credit for the attack.

This is a disaster waiting to happen. Recall that a worst-case-compromised CPU will order every unsafe action that the physical process is physically and electrically able to carry out. Putting networked CPUs into home appliances is a safety hazard. A great many experts are wringing their hands asking how to protect private, personally-identifiable data in the brave new world of IoT. Almost nobody is asking how to protect consumer safety.

The Industrial Internet of Things (IIoT) is this same concept applied to important, complex, and often dangerous industrial processes. Our first instinct might be to ask, "Why is this a good idea?" The answer is that there is simply too much money to be saved and new capabilities to be developed via the IIoT, for the IIoT phenomenon to fade away. When one industrial vendor starts shipping IIoT equipment able to save money or create value in a particular application, other vendors must follow or lose business. The IIoT is the future of SCADA systems, and we must create a way to deal with safety, reliability and security issues.

The IIoT Vision

The vision for the IIoT is compelling and can be paraphrased: imagine a world where a refinery, pharmaceutical plant or power plant has a problem with how the physical, industrial process is being operated. The SCADA people at the plant drive to their nearest distributor and purchase 43 brand new IIoT widgets. They drive back to the plant, connect the widgets to the physical process, and turn them all on.

The widgets connect to the widget vendor's Internet cloud site through a cellular network. That cloud site coordinates with other cloud sites serving other devices at the plant. Since physical industrial equipment and configurations have all been standardized as part of IIoT initiatives, each new IIoT widget quickly "figures out" where it is, what it is connected to, what the problem is, and how to solve it. The new widgets self-configure, self-secure, and "just work." None of this is exceptional – this IIoT plant is managed by plant operators in a remote location, via a cloud-based HMI.

All networks are "flat," meaning everything is on the Internet, talking to the cloud. Everything is secure. Everything just works.

This is a compelling vision. Now – what's wrong with this picture?

The IT guys at the back of the room know. They were the ones asking about the IIoT back in Chapter 5, when we were talking about physical perimeters, cyber perimeters and unidirectional gateways. IT security gurus have been telling us for years that perimeters are dissolving. Where is the physical security perimeter around a cell phone? Where is the cyber perimeter?

Hmm – let's look back and read the IIoT vision statement again. Where is someone trying to sell us a bill of goods? Hint: look for the word "secure."

Recall the nuclear safety system example in Chapter 5. Let's say the problem we need our new IIoT widgets to solve at our plant has to do with safety systems, or with preventing contamination of a product being produced for human consumption. Are we really going to put our brand new, state-of-the-art safety instrumented systems on the open Internet where every attacker on the planet can send attack packets to our equipment with no intervening security measures?

Nothing is secure. All software can be hacked, even "secure" software, and every message can be an attack. What reason can there be to permit every attacker on the planet, no matter how smart or stupid, no matter how capable or not, to test the defenses of our control systems with attack packets all day long? There is no reason. Nobody will ever put important control components on the Internet, no matter how "secure" the vendor says these components are. This is true for the same reason that no industrial site is ever going to allow members of the public to walk up and touch the dials and switches controlling important industrial equipment.

Certain industrial sites or parts of industrial sites will *always* have physical security perimeters. We can hold up "put everything on the Internet" as a goal, but only if we acknowledge that we will never reach that goal. We can however, come much closer to that goal than we are now – this is the opportunity for the IIoT. Precisely how close we can come is an open research question.

For starters, we can put any equipment we want on the Internet provided that, when absolutely everything we put on the Internet is compromised in a worst-case cyber attack, we are still confident that no serious consequences ensue. For example, disposable rainfall meters might be deployed throughout the watershed of a city's water system, meters that are physically unable to control any part of the water system. In addition, the data these meters provide is being correlated with more conventional rainfall measurements, so even the impact of falsified readings is minimal.

When we have strong assurances of the safety and reliability of the industrial process, even in the face of complete compromise of Internet-facing equipment and complete forgery of the monitoring data, then deploying equipment on the Internet becomes a simple cost/benefit decision.

On the other hand, as a rule of thumb, any physical, industrial equipment that is important enough or dangerous enough to warrant a physical security perimeter generally also warrants a cyber security perimeter. If we cannot afford to have members of the public to walk up to and misoperate dangerous or sensitive physical equipment, we generally do not want members of the public sending random attack packets to computers controlling that physical equipment either. Control is not the only risk here. Often we cannot tolerate members of the public sending random attack messages to even those computers that monitor sensitive equipment. This situation may never change – this may well be the future of the IIoT.

To reiterate this important point: safety-critical equipment is generally not the only IIoT equipment worth protecting with physical and cyber-security perimeters. If physical or cyber manipulations can impair the productivity of costly industrial investments, we must deploy physical and cyber perimeters for such equipment as well.

Militarily Strategic Targets

Cloud computing is integral to the IIoT vision, and poses a second, big security problem. IIoT equipment is most frequently useless on its own – IIoT equipment assumes an ability to report data to a central cloud service on the Internet, and IIoT equipment may be controlled by the cloud as well. This makes cloud sites militarily strategic targets, targets that are virtually impossible to secure against the attackers who will sooner or later target the sites.

For example, industrial vendors are starting to sell cloud HMI systems. These systems gather data from SCADA equipment, use encrypted communications to send that data to a cloud site, and make the data available to customers again as HMI renderings. These HMI pictures can be seen on any Internet-connected computer or cell phone.

Isn't this convenient? We can see exactly what our plant operator sees, from anywhere in the world. For an extra fee, we can enable not only monitoring, but we can also control our physical process through these cloud systems as well, from our cell phones. The vendors here claim their cloud systems are "completely secure" because the encrypted connections used to connect the SCADA network to the cloud all originate on the SCADA network. This means that no SCADA firewall rules need to change to enable us to control our gigawatt-scale power plants, from our cell phones, while we are stopped at traffic lights. So we are "perfectly secure."

This is, of course, nonsense.

There are so many things wrong with this picture it is hard to see where to begin. How many guards, gates and guns are deployed around the power plant, and how many are deployed around our cell phones? And what was that nonsense about encrypted connections through firewalls being "completely secure?" A single stolen password will let anyone in the world with a cell phone log into the cloud provider and control our power plant, using the same screens our operators use.

It gets worse. For some time now, many vendors of physical industrial equipment and industrial software have required cloud monitoring and cloud control of customer equipment as a condition of warranties and support contracts. The discussion of turbine vendors in Chapter 10 is just such an example.

These central cloud sites have the ability to continuously monitor and occasionally adjust the physical equipment and control system software, remotely. Central cloud sites maintain VPN or other connections to hundreds or thousands of customer sites simultaneously. These connections permit the vendors' central cloud systems and personnel to monitor systems remotely, and sometimes to control them as well.

In some cases, cloud vendors can also issue remote control commands to their equipment at the site. In other cases, remote desktop or other interactive remote access capabilities are enabled. Some vendors protect these interactive remote access capabilities with a security bypass mechanism of some sort, which must be physically activated by personnel at the customer site. With other vendors, there is no such protection.

What happens then, when even one of these customer sites is compromised? Attacks can flow over encrypted channels just as easily as legitimate communications flow over such channels. Any compromised customer site can attack the central vendor.

What happens when the central vendor site is compromised? This is the site with bi-directional connectivity with computers operating thousands of nearly-identical pieces of powerful, important industrial equipment. When only IT-style protections are used, any compromised customer site can pivot attacks to other customer sites through the central vendor.

A compromised vendor site therefore risks misoperating all of the connected customer sites at once. Such an attack risks utterly crippling one kind of industrial infrastructure throughout a large geography. At best, such an attack would represent a disaster, and at worst a catastrophe. The ability to bring about catastrophic consequences throughout a large geography makes many vendors' cloud sites militarily strategic targets.

Now, IIoT vendors' marketing people all assure us their cloud sites are "secure." Nothing is secure. Do any of us believe that any industrial vendor in the world has the means to "secure" a militarily-strategic site against a military-grade cyber-assault?

Many vendors claim that customers can control their risk, by subscribing to "monitor only" services, instead of "monitor and control." Unfortunately, many vendors configure their connections to customer SCADA systems exactly the same way for "monitor only" services as for "monitor and control" services. In the former case, the vendor simply does not use the control capabilities of these connections when the customer has paid only for monitoring. The capability of the vendor to control the customer's industrial process still exists. Vendors justify this by pointing out that having only a single kind of configuration for equipment deployed at the customer site reduces the vendors' costs.

Worse, even if the vendor claims to have no ability to send control messages to computers at the customer site, and even if there is a secure bypass mechanism preventing on-demand access to remote desktop or similar facilities, the vendor almost always has the ability to issue queries to the vendor's control systems at the customer site. This allows the vendor to retrieve more-detailed diagnostic information when vibration or other physical performance anomalies arise.

The problem here is the third law of SCADA security – every message can be an attack. When a vendor's cloud site is compromised, the ability to send queries to computers at the customer site means the attacker has the ability to send attacks to those control-system computers as well.

The third law also guarantees that any IT-style network connection between a customer site's SCADA system and the cloud vendor's equipment at the industrial site means that attacks can pivot from the cloud to the vendor's equipment at the site, and then from there, through to the customer's SCADA system.

To summarize, today, most cloud vendors' central sites are connected to monitoring and control computers at customer sites across bi-directional, encrypted communications mechanisms. Most of these monitoring and control computers are similarly, bidirectionally, connected to customer SCADA systems. This daisy-chain of bidirectional connections permits attacks to pivot from any compromised customer to the cloud site, and from the cloud site to other customers. In at least some cases, the cloud site has on-demand interactive-remote-access to customer sites, which makes pivoting that much easier.

IIoT Networks

To address these and other security problems of cloud-based IIoT, we consider first what networks exist at a typical industrial site, and how they are interconnected. Most industrial sites, and IIoT sites to an increasing degree, use several kinds of computer networks simultaneously:

- The Internet – wired, wireless and cellular networks where every device has an Internet address, and is reachable directly by every other Internet-connected device on the planet,
- The Corporate IT network – with access to the Internet, email, etc., generally protected by corporate firewalls and corporate IT security systems,
- Control networks – able to communicate directly with computers that monitor and control physical equipment,
- Safety networks – networks of special purpose computers dedicated to preventing injury, loss of life, and environmental disasters, and

- Protection networks – networks of special purpose computers dedicated to preventing damage to costly industrial equipment.

At the most important or most dangerous sites, these networks may not be physically intermingled. At such sites, there may be only one kind of network in each physical area. This reduces opportunities for high-consequence errors and omissions.

More typically, each physical area at an industrial site will be within the physical perimeter of at least two of these networks. For example, cellular connectivity is universal at many industrial sites, and corporate Wi-Fi connections are almost as universal. Control network wiring tends to run almost everywhere within most sites. Safety networks and protection networks tend to be physically smaller than control networks, but wiring for these networks may run through the same conduits as control network wiring, or even corporate network wiring.

IIoT Network Perimeters

To define a network perimeter, we must first decide how to partition/segment our networks. SCADA security advice encourages us to group equipment that has similar security requirements and if misoperated, has similar consequences. Different standards and guidance describe their network segments with different names. Some call them safety-critical, reliability-critical and non-critical, others call them high-impact, medium-impact and low-impact, still others identify numbered security classes or network levels. Most standards prescribe strong network perimeter protection for all but the least-critical network segments.

Note that criticality is often a transitive characteristic. Within a network segment, computers can generally communicate with each other more or less unimpeded, which means attacks can jump or pivot from one compromised computer to another comparatively easily. In many circumstances therefore, all of the computers on a network segment are regarded as being as critical as the most critical computer on the segment, and all must be managed for physical and cyber security as thoroughly as the most critical computer is managed. In addition, when bi-directional message forwarding is enabled between a pair of network segments, many standards demand that both network segments are managed as if they were at the same level of criticality as the most-critical segment.

This latter rule has consequences for IT networks. Since most IT networks routinely exchange electronic mail, web pages, and other messages with the Internet, and since no single entity is able to control the physical or cyber security characteristics of every machine on the Internet, all IT networks must be regarded as being at the same level of security and criticality as the Internet. This effectively rules out hosting reliability-critical or safety-critical functions on computers with access to IT networks.

When segmenting networks, we generally group safety and protection networks together at the highest level of criticality, control networks next, and lump corporate networks together with the Internet at the lowest, non-critical level. Corporate networks may be regarded by IT teams as business-critical, but cannot be regarded by SCADA teams as safety-critical or reliability-critical.

Unidirectional gateway protections should be the only communications permitted between networks at different levels of criticality. When it is impractical to deploy such protections between a pair of networks, the pair of networks must be secured and managed at the highest level of criticality of any equipment on the network. For example, if it is impractical to separate safety and control networks unidirectionally, the entire control network must be protected as though it were a safety network.

As to IIoT equipment, there are two kinds of such equipment: equipment that is physically able to control the physical world, and equipment that is physically able to monitor the world only. The latter can be connected directly to the Internet, provided that safety and reliability engineering studies agree. Such studies must demonstrate that the physical, industrial process will continue to operate sufficiently safely and reliably, even if each and every Internet-exposed IIoT monitoring device is simultaneously compromised. A compromised device may yield inaccurate data, may yield no data at all, and may yield messages that seek to attack other equipment. If the physical consequences of such an attack are acceptable, then go wild: connect the IIoT equipment directly to the Internet or to a cell phone network. If the physical consequences are unacceptable, for example when conclusions based on the monitoring data are communicated back into the SCADA system to control a reliability-critical process automatically, then the monitoring network and indeed the monitoring data are safety-critical or reliability-critical. This means the monitoring equipment and monitoring data must be protected as a SCADA resource.

The same principle applies to IIoT equipment capable of physical control. In practice, it is rare for an engineering study to conclude that the consequences of physical miscontrol are acceptable. In practice, IIoT equipment that is physically able to control an industrial process should almost always be deployed on a network with a unidirectional perimeter.

Unidirectional gateways have no problems sending data out to the cloud for analysis. When anything comes back from the cloud into a control network though, that incoming information must be subjected to the highest levels of scrutiny. Today, most industrial sites are likely to conclude that a "cloud HMI" is an unacceptable risk. At some future date, the risk may be acceptable. What changes between now and then is the amount of information coming back into critical control systems, and the degree of scrutiny to which we can subject that data.

For example, imagine that a remote, cloud HMI is able to send only a very small number of very short, numeric commands into a control system in a manner analogous to the automated remote maintenance systems of Chapter 10. These command codes are not interpreted by individual control devices, but by higher-level SCADA computers. The commands do not instruct individual devices to issue controls to the physical world, but rather select between known-safe operating modes for the physical process.

For example, an electric transmission grid might be configured to operate in "normal" mode most of the time and in a "high-load-emergency" mode for up to 3 hours at a time, 3 times a year. The remote HMI in this example is able to send only a "0" or a "1" into the SCADA system, and nothing else. Operating in a "high-load-emergency" mode during peak load periods can age transformers and other equipment at a slightly accelerated rate, but causes no other damage.

Less extreme examples can be imagined. How much can be controlled remotely, safely, and what supporting systems need to be in place in the IIoT equipment and in perimeter-protected IIoT to permit such control is an open question.

The IT guys at the back of the room are unhappy about this. Can the IT gurus who tell us "the perimeter is dead" all be wrong about SCADA perimeters? Emerging IIoT designs send pretty much everything through cloud systems via the Internet – critical monitoring data, critical control signals, and everything really. Is gazillion-bit encryption and root-of-trust authentication enough to protect such systems?

We all know the answer already: every piece of information can be an attack. Exchanging information with cloud systems allows attacks to flow. Attacks from poorly-defended customers can pivot through cloud systems to well-defended customers. These attacks pass through encrypted connections as easily as plaint-text connections, and root-of-trust systems are no protection from misoperation by legitimate, trusted, but compromised, endpoints.

In all cases, we need to analyze what are the worst-case physical consequences of SCADA networks compromised by IIoT cloud connections. If these consequences are unacceptable, then the "put everything on the Internet" IIoT design is unacceptable, and we need to use a different design.

IIoT Physical Perimeter

At an industrial site where many different networks are deployed at different levels of sensitivity, how are we to prevent human error from compromising our networks – for example, plugging laptops, or cell phones, or USB drives into the wrong connectors? The most sensitive industrial sites deal with this problem all the time, and the solutions are not complex.

In the most dangerous or important areas in a site, or at the very most important industrial sites entire, safety and security designers simply do not permit multiple physical networks, and do not use wireless network equipment at all. There is a physical perimeter around the most important areas of industrial sites, and people are searched as they enter these areas, for their own protection. Cell phones are not permitted, nor are laptops or USB drives.

When such equipment is essential to the operation of the site, known-clean laptops and USB drives can be picked up by personnel once they pass through physical security. This equipment is left behind as people leave the secure area again. Any laptop or USB drive that is ever physically removed from the secure area is regarded as compromised.

In less-dangerous areas, networks may be intermixed. Clear labelling of different classes of networks, and physical protections for the most sensitive connectors, is essential. Device control systems and network access-control systems are no guarantee against nation-state-class attacks, but such systems help, and are strong protections against errors and omissions.

This is especially true if such systems are coupled with rigorous monitoring and follow-up. If every employee who ever plugs a cell phone or laptop into the wrong port is immediately visited by security for a half-hour review of policies, procedures and roles, people learn very quickly to be careful what they plug in, and where. In fact, in organizations with rigorous monitoring and follow-up, it is the rank-and-file employees themselves who demand clear labelling and physical connector protections, to prevent security incidents from being recorded in their own personnel records.

IIoT Cloud Perimeters

Industrial sites need protection from cloud sites, but central cloud sites generally deserve protection as well. Central cloud sites generally both acquire data from equipment that customers deploy, and send something back to the customer as well. Information may be sent back to customer SCADA networks, or into other customer systems, such as their Internet-connected cell phones.

Since information flows both into and out of cloud systems are essential, such systems should be protected by inbound/outbound unidirectional gateways. Such gateways effectively prevent pivoting attacks where compromised customer equipment tries to compromise the cloud site. Such gateways can also prevent a central site compromised by an insider from propagating malware back into thousands of customer networks simultaneously.

What may not be obvious is that to prevent pivoting, a separate gateway pair must be established for each customer, or each customer site, depending on the degree of protection needed. This is because a unidirectional gateway consists of both unidirectional hardware, and software connectors running on conventional computers. If many customers connect to a single computer, that computer may be attacked, compromised, and used to pivot attacks. It makes no difference that the pivot computer is part of a unidirectional gateway or is any other computer. Again, those attacks can generally be pushed back from cloud providers to other customers through VPN or other encrypted connections.

Putting It All Together

How close can we come to the IIoT vision put forward at the beginning of the chapter? Imagine:

- An industrial site – say a refinery – has all types of networks deployed – Corporate IT, wired, cellular, Wi-Fi, SCADA, SIS and protection networks.
- All equipment, wiring and network connectors are clearly labelled as to what class of equipment this is: safety/protection-critical, SCADA/reliability-critical, Corporate IT, or Internet.
- Strong physical security is deployed at the physical boundary of the site. Video monitoring is deployed throughout the site, as is detailed audit logging of computers and networks at the site. Audit logs are stored off-site in a cloud provider. Video recordings are stored on-site in a location accessible to only a handful of trusted physical security personnel.
- Safety/protection and SCADA networks and devices all have rigorously-monitored removable device controls and network access controls deployed.
- Secondary security controls, including pervasive encryption, whitelisting systems, security updates, account management and intrusion detection systems, are deployed on equipment that tolerates such systems.
- Noncritical monitoring equipment that is physically incapable of any sort of physical control is deployed on Wi-Fi, cellular and Internet networks.
- Safety and protection networks are protected by outbound-only unidirectional gateways.
- SCADA networks are protected by inbound/outbound unidirectional gateways.
- All cloud systems used by the site are protected by per-site inbound/outbound unidirectional gateways.
- The site's human operators are all located at the corporate head office, in an inbound/outbound-protected network, connected to a

remote HMI. The physical work-area for the operators enjoys physical and cyber protections equivalent to the protections for SCADA network areas at the refinery.

- Reliability engineering has determined that the risk of downtime due to OPSWAN or Internet connectivity failures is acceptably mitigated by the number of redundant communications connections deployed to the central site, the cloud sites, and the refinery itself.

- IIoT equipment at the plant is configured in local clusters, cooperating to ensure that the plant operates in a very limited number of safe, productive, reliable modes. Remote plant operators can send very limited commands into the site to select between modes, and nothing else. For example, operators can shut down portions of the site and request repair crews to investigate problems, but cannot control individual devices.

- Remote vendor connections are all via outbound-only unidirectional gateways, with remote screen view set up as-needed when vendors need to adjust equipment or systems at the refinery.

What are the residual risks?

- Insiders at the site are still a risk – anyone standing beside important equipment with a hammer, or in a computer room with a screwdriver or a bucket of water, is still a risk. This class of threat is well-understood though, and is managed by personnel adept in physical and personnel security.

- Insiders at cloud sites and at the central corporate site are still a risk, but this risk is limited to remotely instructing the industrial process to act in an incorrect mode. Pivoting from those sites into a unidirectionally-protected SCADA network is only possible with insider assistance at the refinery.

- Malicious vendor personnel, or compromised vendor sites, are unable to misoperate refinery equipment, unless they manage to deceive someone at the refinery into such misoperation during a remote screen view session.

- Safety and protection systems can be compromised only locally and physically, by someone at the industrial site. This dramatically reduces the likelihood of serious consequences of any sort of successful attack, no matter what other residual risks remain.

- Remote control attacks originated by and operated by distant adversaries are effectively impossible without insider assistance.

- Pivoting attacks into the site from the corporate network, a cloud site, or some other site on the Internet are effectively impossible without insider assistance.

- Accidental compromise by common malware or even targeted malware physically carried into a critical network area is extremely unlikely – not just because of the strong cyber perimeter and pervasive removable media/device controls, but also because of the secondary controls deployed throughout much of the infrastructure.

This would seem to be a well-defended IIoT network. It is not "flat" in that there are some strong physical and cyber perimeter defenses deployed, but the network does profit from extensive use of Internet-based communications, vendor connections, cloud analytics and cloud control systems. Many things can be done remotely. The site is operated remotely, and is largely supported remotely.

Summary

Every message can be an attack, and IIoT systems are predicated with bidirectional exchanges of information with central cloud systems. Central cloud systems can be militarily-strategic targets, when such systems enable simultaneous compromise of large numbers of physical systems. No matter what cloud vendors say, when a cloud site is a military target, there is nothing the site can do to prevent eventual compromise.

To prevent a site from becoming such a target, the ability of an attacker to pivot from the compromised cloud site must be defeated. This can be accomplished by deploying inbound / outbound unidirectional gateways at the cloud site, one per customer. This can also be accomplished by deploying gateways at IIoT customer sites as perimeter protections between networks at different levels of criticality. Note again, that this does not serve to defend the site against a military-grade attacker. These measures serve to render the site unable to attack many customer sites simultaneously, and so renders the site useless as a military target.

To say "the perimeter is dead" about IIoT sites is wrong. Physical and network perimeters are essential to safe and reliable operations. The benefits of IIoT deployments are realizable, but only with essential physical and network perimeters deployed.

Recommended Reading

The Industrial Internet of Things Security Framework, 2016, by the Industrial Internet Consortium

"It is a pain in the ass waiting around
for someone to try to kill you."
-- Roger Zelazny, Trumps of Doom, 1986

Chapter 13 – Advanced Topics

Chapter 12's evaluation of an acceptably-secure IIoT installation was based on modern-day threats. There are other risks, considered emerging threats.

Emerging threats distress many. Brand new cyber-sabotage attacks different from any seen before seem to be invented daily. This is alarming, costly and annoying to people charged with keeping SCADA security defenses current. The constant stream of new kinds of attacks makes our goals as defenders appear impossible to achieve.

What is possible though, really depends on the correct formulation of our goals. Nothing can ever be "secure." It is however, both possible and affordable to defeat, reliably, all attackers except those willing to spend ruinous sums of money, time and talent to attack us.

So, how should we interpret this constant barrage of attacks we have never seen before? It turns out that the "newness" of these attacks is an illusion. There is only one way to sabotage an industrial site, and that is to somehow transport attack information past the site's perimeter.

Most new attacks target IT networks. IT networks have necessarily porous network and physical perimeters – electronic mail must enter the network constantly, as must web pages and other content. To be successful against IT-class defenses, new IT attacks need only to find yet another way to defeat the automatic filtering software deployed on high-volume IT/Internet connections. This is a problem for IT network defenders, and for SCADA systems defended with only IT-class protections. This is not a problem for properly-protected SCADA networks.

Each of the much smaller number of new attacks relevant to SCADA systems protected with prevention-centric approaches is simply an indication of our enemies desperately trying to find some new kind of trick to transmit an attack past our now thoroughly-protected perimeter. Our enemies need some way of packaging the attack into information, and some way of transmitting that information past our perimeter security systems.

We look at a number of "new" and current topics of discussion.

Hardware Supply Chain

When brand new computer equipment is purchased and shipped to an industrial site, that equipment must be inspected. We must ensure that the computing and communications hardware contains only those functions we specified. Nation-state adversaries have been known to intercept computer shipments from hardware vendors and insert unauthorized wireless and other transmitters in the equipment. This enables remote operation of the compromised equipment once the computers are deployed at a destination site. Such equipment may show no obvious signs of tampering when the attackers have repackaged, re-shrink-wrapped, and otherwise made their tampered-with equipment seem in "brand new" condition.

Such tampering can be particularly difficult to recognize as computer technology advances. For example, every USB device contains a CPU, memory and information storage hardware, from the humblest flash stick, mouse or keyboard, to the most sophisticated industrial sensors. A USB mouse purchased at the local computer store could include compromised firmware, or even malicious wireless communications hardware. The CPU in the mouse might report "yes I am a mouse" when connected to a computer, but then 12 hours later, presumably in the dead of night, report "whoops – I'm also a keyboard, and a flash stick." The mouse could then start issuing keyboard commands to the connected computer, transferring remote-control malware to the computer and activating the malware. Physically disassembling USB equipment and inspecting the devices' programming can be very difficult. Physically disassembling and inspecting CPU and other chips is not only extremely difficult, but most often physically destroys the chip being inspected.

All of these issues are at the heart of today's "supply chain integrity" debates, which seek to establish "trusted supply chains," from chip designers and manufacturers all the way through to the shipping companies that deliver product to end users. This is a very difficult problem to solve. This issue is the reason many nations' militaries strongly prefer to source their most important weapons and supporting technologies from "trusted" local suppliers. The problem with this approach is that the most modern components tend to have a large number of suppliers. Trust is most easily betrayed when that trust depends on the reliable behavior of each of thousands or tens of thousands of individuals in a large supply chain.

To help address this problem, research efforts are under way to characterize "involuntary" behaviors of hardware systems – everything from electromagnetic emissions to fine-grained characteristics of power usage. In theory, such involuntary behaviors can be used to determine whether equipment has been tampered with. In practice, this is still an emerging field of research. We are only starting to understand what measurements we might make and how to make them. We understand even less whether our enemies might be able to sabotage chip or hardware designs in ways that defeat one or another kind of passive "involuntary" monitoring systems.

Research is also starting to consider "manufacture on demand" systems using local 3-D printers to create circuit boards or even simple chips. These systems would convert software into custom hardware, eliminating the CPU, software, and software vulnerabilities from some control system components. Today, such approaches are entirely impractical for all but the very simplest software components.

In short, we cannot count on any of this research to help us any time soon. Today's best primary preventive measures against this type of threat are physical inspection of equipment coming into the SCADA system and a trusted supply chain.

Note that IT-style secondary measures are not effective either, against this class of threat. Any enemy able to insert wireless communications equipment into servers destined for our SCADA system is not likely to use those communications to launch antivirus-detectable malware against us. Similarly, if our enemy is this sophisticated, they will not limit themselves to the use of known vulnerabilities that security update programs might address, nor will they limit themselves to attacks that network intrusion-detection signatures can identify.

Deploying these secondary systems does help to some degree. For example, such systems might catch a contractor using a low-tech attack, such as duct-taping a Wi-Fi-capable laptop underneath a computer near the bottom of a rack, in order to provide the contractor with a remote-control platform for attacking the network. That a duct-taped-laptop attack is even possible though, represents a failure of what should be our primary preventive measures, namely screening of untrusted third parties and supervision of them while they are on site.

Software Supply Chain

When discussing supply chain issues, the software supply chain is of concern as well. Software permitted into a SCADA network can contain anything from inadvertent safety and reliability defects, to remote control malware or even autonomous Stuxnet-class malware. This software may come directly from a software vendor, or may have passed through the hands of one or more intermediate value-added resellers, systems integrators, or service providers. Verifying the integrity of software is very difficult. For example:

- Software product downloads are frequently accompanied by cryptographic signatures to permit people who are downloading the files to detect tampering. The obvious way to defeat this approach is for an adversary to tamper with both the download file and the posted signatures, so that the posted signatures match the malicious download file. In short, even if we as customers of SCADA vendors trust the vendor and all of their software developers and QA teams, can we trust that those vendors' websites have not been compromised?

- Worse, our vendors themselves may not be trustworthy. Insiders planted in the vendors' software development teams or QA teams can insert malware or other capabilities into products during development. When the modified software version is posted for download, it is the vendors' own QA team who calculates product signatures for the compromised product version.

- Either of these attacks can be applied to software vendors' own suppliers. Modern SCADA products frequently contain third-party libraries and sub-components, each of which could have been attacked in this way. We as SCADA customers may prefer to purchase products from large control system vendors, in hopes that large vendors have better-than-average security systems. Attackers though, may prefer to target the smallest and least-well-secured technology and service suppliers serving those large vendors, in order to compromise the vendors' products.

- SCADA sites frequently use systems integrators. These are services providers who acquire hardware and software for the site for both the smallest and the largest projects, configure that hardware and software to the site's specifications, test those configurations, and ultimately transport them to the site for installation and commissioning. These services providers are often easier targets than the SCADA sites themselves. Worse, new versions of SCADA systems brought to our sites by services providers can be large and difficult to inspect.

For example, the Stuxnet malware is widely thought to have been introduced into the Natanz uranium enrichment site by a compromised services provider, in the context of a Siemens S7 project file. These Siemens project files are typical of SCADA system configurations – the files contain up to hundreds of megabytes of code and binary data. Reliably detecting deliberately-hidden malware in this large, complex mix of standard code, custom code and automatically-generated code can be made arbitrarily difficult by developers of the most sophisticated malware.

At present, the best protections in this realm are labor-intensive. We can and should demand that our software vendors and our services providers use strong security measures themselves. When we do not have the means to persuade our vendors to secure themselves properly, for example when the technology vendor is a very large and inflexible organization, we must carefully inspect the software delivered by those suppliers.

Sandboxing, antivirus systems and other automatic inspection techniques can detect a large fraction of common malware, but are much less likely to detect sophisticated, targeted attacks. This leaves only manual inspection and even reverse engineering, but such inspections are only as good as the people carrying out the inspection, and can be prohibitively expensive. Signed software can increase confidence that software has not been modified in transit, but signing systems can be defeated by compromising vendors, stealing signing keys as Stuxnet's authors did, and by exploiting vulnerabilities in signing systems, as Flame's authors did.

Addressing software supply-chain risk more reliably is a topic of on-going research. A perennial call to return to smaller, simpler systems whose security and safety are easier to verify is starting to draw the attention of security researchers. This call in the past was dismissed as a nostalgic view of past SCADA systems, ignoring how costly and inflexible such systems were. Modern researchers are starting to ask how to reap the benefits of today's feature-full, comparatively cheap and immensely powerful software in such a way as to capture, package and deploy only a small number of small, more easily verifiable software artifacts.

Currently, inspection techniques for incoming software include offline scans of physical equipment, hard drives, USB drives and any other artifact able to host software. These scans seek to identify software artifacts and check for vendor signatures, or evaluate those software artifacts using reputation-based systems. Vendor signatures are authentication information software vendors provide to assure customers that the vendors' software has arrived at the customer site un-modified. Reputation-based systems calculate cryptographic checksums for every unit of software. The systems use the checksums to identify how many copies of every unit of software have been observed by these reputation systems in the past. Software that is in widespread use without having been identified as malware, or compromised, has a better reputation than software in very limited use, or software that has never been seen before.

Note that, just as we saw in the most sophisticated hardware supply-chain attacks, the obvious secondary security measures have little value against software supply-chain attacks. If our enemies are clever enough to hide attacks so thoroughly they defeat the automatic software scanners that are our primary preventive measures, they are very likely clever enough to avoid using known vulnerabilities and to deceive intrusion detection systems as well.

Exotic Attacks

In principle, any technology able to communicate information across a physical perimeter, or past a cyber perimeter, can be used to communicate malware into a SCADA network. Exotic attacks in this regard continue to be published. None of these attacks are unexpected in hindsight, because all are variations on perimeter-crossing attacks. For example:

- Many computers, even many SCADA server-class computers, are equipped with a speaker and microphone. This audio equipment is often capable of signaling and receiving frequencies that are out of the range of human hearing. Malicious hardware or software can be deliberately seeded into sensitive equipment, or inserted as part of a supply-chain compromise. Such malware has been proven able to use inaudible audio signaling mechanisms to communicate past network perimeter protections.

- Data can be communicated through electric power lines, and power-line signaling is used routinely for older X-10 home automation equipment. More modern power-line signaling is used by some SCADA systems to communicate with distant substations in an electric grid. This means SCADA computers compromised with power-line signaling capabilities can exchange remote control commands and responses through electric cables.

In practice, these exotic attacks have a very limited physical range, and depend on either a serious supply chain breach, or the active assistance of compromised insiders at a site. It is generally more useful for SCADA sites to invest in security for hardware, software and services supply chains, as well as compromised insiders, than it is to make any investment to address these exotic attacks specifically.

Shared Equipment Attacks

Increased use of cost-saving physical technologies in SCADA systems can pose security threats:

- Keyboard-Video-Mouse (KVM) equipment allows many computers to share one video monitor, keyboard and mouse. This equipment is frequently used to save space in crowded SCADA server rooms. When different computers connected to the same KVM are at different levels of criticality, this is a problem. Researchers have demonstrated ways to communicate remote control commands and responses between computers through KVM equipment.

- Virtualization allows many logical computers to share one physical server or blade server. Virtualization saves computing costs, and simplifies restoring damaged or compromised virtual

135

computers from backups. However, when virtual computers hosted on the same physical computer or blade system connect to networks at different criticality levels, attacks can jump from computer to computer, and from network to network, no matter what strong, unidirectional protections might be in place. Virtual machine systems are software, and all software can be hacked.

These attacks are easily dealt with. Permit no sharing of physical equipment between networks and computers at different levels of criticality – not KVMs or virtual hosts, not uninterruptable power supplies or even electric circuits.

Wiring

Physical communications wiring at an industrial site is hardly a new attack, but awareness of risks due to wiring is increasing, as the criticality of perimeter defenses is becoming better understood.

Most industrial sites are mazes of hundreds of kilometers of wiring. A single deliberate, or mistaken, cross-connection between a SCADA network and a less-critical network is an opportunity for attacks to flow into the SCADA network. The usual preventive precautions here include:

- Physical security, visitor/contractor escort systems and video monitoring are all standard deterrents to intruders deliberately changing wiring inside a security perimeter.
- Training and awareness to alert site personnel to the dangers of cross-connecting networks. Training and awareness includes color-coding or otherwise labelling wiring for different kinds of networks that must not be interconnected.

Secondary protections can help as well. Encryption / authentication systems can prevent equipment on different networks from interacting, even if there is a cross-connection. Network Access Controls can also help prevent such interactions. Intrusion detection systems that monitor what machines are visible on a network can catch almost all accidental interconnections.

In addition, periodic wiring inventories, especially of wiring crossing physical security perimeters, have value in enforcing security perimeters. Carrying out such a physical inventory can represent a significant cost, but the investment can yield more than just security value. Not only does a wiring inventory identify unauthorized wiring, it can also verify engineering diagrams and increase our confidence in our own understanding of what wiring is deployed at our sites and how our SCADA networks work.

For example, well-meaning hardware vendors installing their equipment at a site often install their own telephone, Internet or other wiring into their equipment to facilitate central "monitoring and diagnostics" services. Every such connection that bypasses unidirectional and other cyber-perimeter protections is a threat. Once a wiring inventory is complete and a security program is established, our primary preventive measure should be strict supervision of contractors on site and a thorough inspection of new installations and wiring before going live with those installations.

Wireless Networks

Wireless networks are less of an emerging threat and more of a perennial source of confusion and debate. Wireless networks generally cost much less to establish than wired networks, and so are used increasingly at SCADA sites. Using wireless networks for critical control functions is therefore tempting, and is a topic of continued debate in both IIoT and non-IIoT contexts. A number of security risks are unique to wireless networks, and some of these risks are often neglected by industrial sites.

To start with, all wireless communications are uniquely vulnerable to "denial of service" attacks that disable wireless communications. For example, wallet-sized wireless signal jammers are available for purchase on the Internet. These devices transmit noise on Wi-Fi frequencies and can disable Wi-Fi communications in a large area for as long as the jammers' batteries last. Wi-Fi directional antennae are also available. A high-intensity jammer with a highly-directional antenna can be mounted in a distant apartment or a vehicle, disrupting communications from kilometers away. Engineering studies of wireless safety and reliability must consider the risk that these attack capabilities pose. These teams must also consider that deterrents to jamming attacks are not likely to be effective, because it is unlikely that distant attackers will be apprehended and prosecuted.

There are other wireless vulnerabilities. Unencrypted and weakly encrypted wireless communications are trivially compromised. Control equipment accessible through such communications is equally trivially misoperated and/or compromised. Again, this misoperation can happen at a distance when the attacker has a cheap, high-gain, directional antenna.

Even if wireless communications use strong encryption, all software can be hacked, even the software running in wireless routers. Worse, wireless communications keys and passwords are stolen as easily as any other keys and passwords. Stolen keys let a distant attacker with a directional antenna misoperate or compromise equipment reachable through wireless communications.

What is often not considered by teams considering wireless media for critical communications is that there is a risk that certain kinds of wireless communications can be hacked from very far away – even the other side of the planet. Many practitioners imagine that all direct attacks on wireless communications must occur at least somewhat locally to the target, within the range of an antenna. This is not so.

For all these reasons, the most cautious industrial sites refuse to use wireless communications for anything more important than cellular phone calls and Internet browsing. On the other hand, wireless communications may be the only practical way to communicate at all over long distances with very remote sites.

Fundamentally, anyone deploying wireless communications at industrial sites needs to be aware of the security issues that come with such communications, and must deploy primary preventive security measures to prevent unacceptable compromise conditions. For example, if wireless communications with a remote site are absolutely essential, deploying unidirectional gateway technologies at the remote site can limit the consequences of compromised Wi-Fi communications.

Periodic inventories of wireless communications at industrial sites can help as well, but such inventories can be costly, and are secondary, detective measures, not primary, preventive measures. Wireless inventories can be much more difficult to carry out than wired communications inventories, because wireless communications can occur on a wide range of frequencies, and may transmit a detectable signal only when a covert transmitter is actively sending messages. When transmitters are silent for long periods between burst-type transmissions, covert transmitters may be very difficult to detect and locate.

Summary

New attacks are invented constantly. New IT-class attacks are constant threats to networks defended with only IT-class protections. New attacks on prevention-centric industrial sites are much less common, and are essentially all variations on a theme: invent some new way to cross the perimeter. Strong, perimeter-centric protections go a long way to anticipate these attacks and defeat them before they are invented.

Equipment-sharing and wiring attacks are more mundane, but often overlooked. No physical equipment should be shared between networks and computers at different levels of criticality. All shared assets have the potential to provide covert channels to communicate remote-control attacks between assets at different levels of criticality. Wiring for network segments at different levels of criticality must be clearly labelled and tightly controlled to prevent accidental or malicious interconnections.

Wireless communications are a perennial source of debate. The most safety-conscious and reliability-conscious sites avoid wireless communications for critical networks. Any site considering wireless communications for reliability-critical networks must consider very carefully threats such as encryption credential theft and long-range directional antennas.

Recommended Reading

Youtube recordings of presentations at the *SCADA Security Scientific Symposium (S4)*, 2007-2016, by Digital Bond

SCADA Security

"Endings, to be useful, must be inconclusive."

- - Samuel R. Delany,
Journals written while composing The Einstein Intersection, 1967

Chapter 14 – Wrapping It Up

To review: the essential SCADA security question is "how should we protect our SCADA networks?" We ask the question within the context of the three laws of SCADA security: nothing is secure, all software can be hacked, and every piece of information can be an attack.

IT-centric defense in depth is a failure. This advice tells us to use costly, vulnerable, software-based technologies including strong encryption, antivirus systems, central password management, security update programs, firewalls, network access controls and intrusion detection systems. When using the IT approach, many practitioners believe we can afford to be a bit sloppy with our physical security, our removable media controls, and our transient equipment controls. For example, if a common virus arrives on a USB stick, we imagine that our antivirus systems will catch it. The problem with this IT-centric defense in depth is that sophisticated remote-control and other attacks routinely defeat all of these IT security mechanisms.

A preventive / protective approach to SCADA security is in many senses the exact opposite of the failed defense-in-depth advice. What are secondary controls in IT-centric circles – unidirectional gateways, physical security, physical inspections, strong removable media, and transient device controls – are primary controls in a SCADA-centric approach to security. What are very costly primary controls in the IT-centric approach – security updates, layers of firewalls, intrusion detection systems and practiced incident response teams – are secondary controls in the SCADA-centric approach.

The best SCADA-centric advice tells us to use unidirectional gateways to defeat remote control attacks completely, and to apply high degrees of scrutiny to anything passing through physical perimeters into the SCADA system. Use of removable media on anything except the physical perimeter's malware scanning equipment should be impossible for all well-meaning insiders. Use of unauthorized computers on critical networks should be similarly impossible. These measures reliably defeat remote control attacks, attacks by corporate insiders, and all but deliberate attacks by the most capable SCADA insiders.

We can and should still deploy weaker IT-centric security measures in addition to these strong, primary OT-centric measures, but we should scale our investments in such measures to reflect the return we expect from them. These secondary measures address residual risks of errors and omissions – they will not catch sophisticated compromised SCADA insiders coming after us.

The best risk-management systems focus on physical consequences and attack paths. Business decision-makers understand consequences and attacks far better than they do fictional LFHI incident probabilities, or subjective qualitative numbers. SCADA security maturity models are currently useless, because they measure process, not results. The problem with maturity models is that there is not yet a consensus that the IT-centric defense-in-depth approach has failed us. Until there is such a consensus, organizations using that failed approach can be awarded high maturity results, even though their defensive posture is poor.

Interactive remote access – the kind that lets us reprogram our control systems from our cell phones at traffic lights or from our laptops in our hotel rooms – poses an unacceptable risk. If we can use such systems, so can our enemies. More-secure remote access options exist with almost all of the business benefits of undisciplined IT-style remote access.

In this book, we argue that for most industrial sites, and certainly, for critical infrastructure sites, the bar should be set at least this high: effective attacks on our important SCADA systems should be ruinously expensive and difficult. More specifically, no attacker sipping coffee on another continent should be able to compromise our SCADA systems. No accident of connectivity or removable media should be able to compromise our SCADA systems. Only the most sophisticated supply-chain-based or deliberately-cooperating, compromised SCADA insider attacks should have any chance of breaching the primary defenses we have deployed. The only attacks that should have any chance at all of succeeding against our SCADA systems should be physical attacks. Our enemies really should be forced to put their own lives and liberty at risk when they attack us.

That said, experience proves that a large fraction of IT security practitioners will remain unmoved by this advice and by the OT-centric, preventive approach to SCADA security. There can be many reasons for this. IT practitioners may fear losing responsibility for and control of cyber-security initiatives in an organization, or they may simply be familiar with the "hammer in their hand" and reflexively resist change.

Organizations with SCADA systems must find ways to overcome this resistance. For example, some organizations rotate IT and OT cyber security personnel through each other's responsibilities and physical sites. Working 8 hours a day, 5 days a week inside the kill zone of a worst-case industrial security incident has done wonders for some IT practitioners' perspectives.

SCADA security standards have been evolving very recently to reflect this preventive approach. American nuclear security standards [23] make deploying firewalls so difficult that American nuclear generators have unanimously elected to deploy unidirectional gateways. Canadian nuclear standards [24] and the more general French ANSSI critical infrastructure standards forbid firewalled connections from the most critical networks to less-critical networks. All of these standards demand strict removable media and transient device controls as well. North American NERC CIP standards recognize the strength of unidirectional gateways by exempting power utilities who deploy the gateways at large power plants and high-voltage substations from roughly one third of the CIP requirements [32].

Nothing is secure. This is not, however, a reason to do nothing. We must decide how secure we need our SCADA systems to be, what classes of attacks we must defeat reliably, and we must deploy security systems with the required capabilities. The average SCADA site may not have the resources to defeat military-grade attacks that use compromised insiders, but we can and should reliably defeat any less-resourceful attacker.

With that said, we can certainly make life difficult for even military-grade attackers. We can and should defend our SCADA systems so thoroughly that even our most resourceful enemies come to tear their hair out and curse the names of our security designers. Strong SCADA security is possible and practical, and is cheaper than IT approaches to security that have been force-fit into SCADA systems. There is no excuse for the unacceptably-exposed SCADA systems that we see deployed all over the world.

The means are available. The time is now.

Glossary of Terms and Technologies

Active Directory (AD) – A Microsoft product that manages passwords, security policies and other configurations for a network of computers.

AD – See Active Directory.

ADC – See application data control.

administrative privileges – An account or application with permission to change everything on a computer or device.

advanced, persistent threat (APT) – See targeted persistent attack.

Agence nationale de la sécurité des systèmes d'information (ANSSI) – The French national authority for cyberdefense and network information security.

analog – The opposite of digital – for example, mechanical or electrical switches, gauges and dials.

analog signaling – Any communication mechanism that does not use a series of binary "1" or "0" bits to communicate values. The most common analog signaling mechanism in SCADA systems encodes a measurement or control value in a 4-20mA current loop.

anomaly-based intrusion-detection system – An intrusion-detection system that in some sense learns what "normal" behavior is for a computer, network or other system, and raises alerts when the system behaves outside of these learned, normal bounds. *Limitations:* Most intrusion-detection systems are software, and contain vulnerabilities that may be exploited. In addition, most anomaly-based systems learn that normal system behavior is a range of measured values, such as network usage or memory usage. The most common attack on anomaly-based intrusion-detection system is a "slow" attack, one that changes learned values only slightly, staying within the limits the anomaly-based system has learned are normal.

ANSSI – See Agence nationale de la sécurité des systèmes d'information.

application control – A security technology that maintains a list of applications and libraries that are permitted to execute on a particular computer, and takes measures to block execution of unapproved code. *Limitations:* Application control systems are software and contain vulnerabilities that may be exploited. In addition, application control systems are unable to prevent execution of many scripted attacks, and can be vulnerable to software update attacks. Specifically, all application control systems must have some way to update the list of allowed executables when software version updates and security updates are applied. When an attacker can embed malware in what otherwise appears to be a legitimate update, the application control system will add that malware to the list of allowed executables.

application data control (ADC) – Policy-based control over OT data in motion through unidirectional gateways.

APT – See advanced, persistent threat.

attack – Any deliberate destruction or misoperation of physical equipment. See cyber attack.

attack modelling – Communicating security postures to business decision makers by describing representative attacks and consequences.

authentication – Any mechanism that serves to identify messages from legitimate sources. Most commonly: a signed, cryptographic hash code.

anti virus (AV) – Strictly speaking: a system that matches applications, libraries and other executables to a library of rules or "signatures." When a match is found, the executable code is flagged as suspect, and most often set aside or "quarantined" to prevent further execution. More generally, modern, integrated antivirus products tend to have features of other products as well. For example, they may apply rules to network communications, similar to network intrusion-detection systems, and may look for anomalous patterns of code executing on hosts as well. *Limitations:* AV systems are software, have vulnerabilities and so can be hacked. Malware can try to turn off AV checking, but modern AV products take measures to make this difficult to do. The simplest way to defeat AV is to write new malware that the AV system has never seen before, and for which the AV system has no signatures.

AV – See anti virus.

black-box – Any artifact whose inner workings are not evident to an external examiner. Common usage in security contexts is as an adjective applied to some sort of examination or test. Used this way, it means the examination or test starts with access only to information the system itself advertises, or information about the system that was previously published to accessible sources. For example: a penetration test by a tester with no pre-existing access to target system designs. See also: white box.

botnet – A collection of compromised computers under the remote control of a central computer or computers.

buffer-overflow – An attack where larger-than-expected messages or message fields are sent to a computer. The computer software mistakenly writes the too-large data into memory, over-writing memory areas adjacent to the memory intended to store the data. Done carefully, this kind of attack can result in the target computer executing instructions in the attack itself, which is generally the first step in causing the compromised computer to download remote-access-class malware.

cloud computing – Using distant, or Internet-based, computers to store, analyze or otherwise process data.

command and control center – A computer with remote control of other compromised computers.

compensating measures – Security measures implemented to address software or system vulnerabilities that cannot be remediated directly.

compromised computer – Any computer doing our enemy's bidding in addition to or instead of our own.

control system – Any system of computers that is able to control one or more aspects of a physical process. See also: SCADA system.

criticality boundary – A connection between networks where the consequences of compromise differ dramatically between the networks.

current loop – An analog signaling mechanism that encodes values according to how much current is flowing through an electric circuit. Unlike voltage-based signaling, current-loop signaling degrades very little over long distances.

cyber attack – Any deliberate misoperation of computer equipment.

cyber perimeter – The logical boundary separating the "inside" of a protected SCADA network from the "outside." See also: unidirectional gateway and firewall.

cyber security – The degree to which a computer system resists unauthorized operation.

DBT – See design-basis threat.

device control – Software to prevent most or all uses of removable media, such as CD-ROMs and DVDs, as well as most or all uses of removable devices, such as USB drives, on a computer. *Limitations:* Device control is software. All software has vulnerabilities, and can be subverted. Attacks on device control systems include custom firmware on USB devices to launch USB-communications attacks on connected computers, and forging device identifiers or mechanisms to distinguish allowed from forbidden devices.

data exfiltration – Unauthorized movement of data from a protected network to an external destination.

deep packet inspection – A feature of modern firewalls that supports firewall rules applied to the contents of data packets for a wide variety of IT protocols, providing an IT analogue of unidirectional application data control.

design-basis threat (DBT) – A description of the most capable adversary whose attacks a site is required to defeat with a high degree of confidence.

digital – Computerized – the opposite of "analog."

encryption – Encoding information so that only authorized parties can read the information.

firewall – A router with a filter, deployed routinely between networks at similar levels of criticality, such as between a corporate IT network and the Internet, or internally within SCADA networks. *Limitations:* Firewalls are software and contain vulnerabilities that may be exploited. Firewalls are not recommended to separate safety-critical or reliability-critical networks from less-critical networks. The simplest way to bypass a firewall is to steal its administrative password, log in and reconfigure it. The best-known way is to craft a packet that matches a firewall rule configured to permit traffic from a non-critical network to a critical one.

firmware – Software built into the hardware of a computer system. Firmware is most often stored in read-only-memory chips, or flash memory built into a device.

flip – A type of unidirectional gateway whose orientation can reverse on a schedule.

fuzzing – A kind of semi-automatic message-based attack. Legitimate messages in some communications protocol are changed in semi-random ways, so that the messages are no longer valid messages. Large numbers of different kinds of these variants are sent to a target computer, and the computer is observed. When the computer crashes or otherwise malfunctions, the recent message stream is replayed and examined to determine which variant caused the malfunction.

gazillion – Any unreasonably-large number.

generating unit – A set of equipment in an electric power plant focused on a single generator. For example, in a coal-fired plant, each generating unit is a single furnace, boiler, steam turbine and generator. In a hydro plant, a generating unit is a water turbine and generator.

historian – See process historian.

HMI – See human-machine interface.

honeypot – A computer pretending to be an attack target, designed to lure attacks as part of detection and analysis efforts. *Limitations:* no emulation of a real system is perfect. When attackers or malware artifacts detect that they are interacting with a honeypot, they may call off the attack or take other measures to avoid detection.

human-machine interface – A software system used by a control system operator to summarize, visualize and control large numbers of sensors and actuators in an industrial control system.

inbound / outbound gateways – A pair of unidirectional gateways. One gateway is oriented to replicate servers from a protected SCADA network to an external network, and another, independent unidirectional gateway is oriented to transmit control information from that external network into the SCADA network. *Limitations:* the most sophisticated attackers can propagate malware into a protected network, but then are working blind. Establishing bidirectional control of a protected network requires assistance from an insider at the targeted site.

ICCP – See Inter-Control-Center Protocol.

ICS – See industrial control system.

IDS – See intrusion detection system

industrial control system (ICS) – Any control system able to control an industrial process.

industrial process – Any important, complex and/or dangerous physical process.

information technology (IT) – Hardware and software routinely found on business networks. For example: accounting systems, enterprise resource management systems, human resources systems, file servers, printers, and Internet firewalls.

interactive remote access – A person operating a computer remotely, by moving the mouse and typing on the keyboard.

Inter-Control-Center Protocol (ICCP) – The SCADA communications protocol used to communicate between control centers in an electric grid.

intrusion-detection system (IDS) – Any system that seeks to identify suspicious behavior in computers, networks or other cyber-systems, and raises alerts when such behavior is detected. See anomaly-based intrusion-detection system and signature-based intrusion detection system.

intrusion-prevention system – An intrusion detection system that, when it discovers what may be suspicious behavior, takes measures to block further execution of suspect malware, or further communications on suspect network sessions. *Limitations:* intrusion-prevention systems are software, contain vulnerabilities, and so can be compromised. Any attack that defeats an IDS also defeats the associated intrusion-prevention system, if any. In addition, attackers can often disrupt communications with legitimate computer and network components by issuing packets that appear to be attack packets originating on those legitimate components.

IT – See information technology.

LAN – See local area network.

local area network (LAN) – Any network enclosed entirely within an industrial site's physical security perimeter.

malware – Malicious software. For example: worms, viruses, trojans, or botnets.

NAC – See network access control.

network access control (NAC) – Any system that restricts participation in network communications to approved devices. The most common such technologies are built into managed switches. These switches restrict communications through the switch to devices with approved MAC addresses. *Limitations:* NAC systems are software and contain vulnerabilities that may be exploited. NAC is not considered a strong security control suitable for partitioning safety-critical or reliability-critical networks from less-critical networks, but can be useful for reducing errors where equipment is connected to critical networks incorrectly. The simplest way to attack most NAC systems is to steal the password and reconfigure the system.

operations technology (OT) – Hardware and software routinely found on SCADA or "operations" networks. For example: human-machine interfaces, device communications servers, alarm systems, process historian databases, file servers and printers.

OPC – A standard programming interface to industrial devices and systems. This programming interface is routinely accessed remotely using Microsoft DCOM remote procedure calls, and so is often thought of as a communications protocol as well.

operator – The person using a SCADA system HMI to operate a physical process.

OT – See operations technology.

perimeter – A logical or physical boundary separating "inside" from "outside." See also: cyber perimeter, physical perimeter.

phishing – Email that seeks to deceive a recipient into activating malware attachments, or divulging credentials

physical perimeter – A logical or physical boundary separating the "inside" of an industrial site from the "outside." Physical protections deployed at the perimeter typically include fencing, gates, guards, locks, card-swipe systems, and video monitoring.

pivot – Using a compromised computer to attack other computers, often other computers deeper into layers of networks in a defensive architecture.

primary defenses – Defensive measures designed as the first line of defense against attacks.

process historian – A database optimized to store and manipulate large amounts of time-sequenced data, such as sensor readings from an industrial process.

protection equipment – Industrial devices monitoring sensors in an industrial process, and triggering automatic actions to bring the system back into a safe state when sensors or combinations of sensors ever exceed designated limits. Protection equipment is designed to prevent damage to industrial equipment.

protective relay – A device that monitors sensors in an electrical system, and signals an electric breaker to interrupt current to a part of the system when designated limits are exceeded. Protective relays are designed primarily to prevent damage to industrial equipment, and secondarily to protect safety. Many conditions able to pose threats to industrial equipment can also pose threats to personnel safety and environmental integrity.

ransomware – Malicious software that encrypts files on a computer and demands money in exchange for the cryptographic key that will restore the file contents.

RAT – See remote administration tool.

remote administration tool (RAT) – Malicious software that provides a remote attacker with administrative privileges on a compromised computer.

removable media – Any digital storage medium. For example: CD-ROMs, DVDs, USB drives, floppy disks, and almost all cell phones.

residual risk – Any risk an organization chooses to accept, rather than mitigate or transfer. The residual risk to which an organization is exposed is a measure of how secure that organization is.

router – A device that forwards messages.

server – A computer used primarily to interact with other computers, rather than with a person. Servers often operate at near-maximum load, continuously. Contrast with workstation.

Safety Instrumented System (SIS) – An industrial device or cooperating set of devices monitoring sensors in an industrial process, and triggering automatic actions to bring the system back into a safe state when sensors or combinations of sensors ever exceed designated limits. The safe state is most commonly a complete shutdown of the industrial process. SIS equipment is designed to protect human life and environmental integrity.

safety program – A set of policies, procedures and technologies designed to protect human life and environmental integrity.

sandbox – A virtual machine in which complex files are opened by their respective applications. The virtual clock on the machine is advanced, and other measures are taken to try to stimulate the activity of any embedded malware. The virtual machine is then monitored to try to detect the operation of malware. For example, does the machine send messages to the Internet, or create unexpected files anywhere in the filesystem? *Limitations:* Malware authors have started producing sandbox-aware malware that detects that it is operating in a sandbox and carries out none of the usual suspicious activities when a sandbox is detected. Malware authors have also demonstrated the ability to exploit vulnerabilities in the sandbox mechanism to escape from the sandbox and infect the computer running the sandbox.

SCADA system – See Supervisory Control and Data Acquisition system.

secure shell (ssh) – An application that issues commands to a remote machine, and receives their responses, over an encrypted network connection. *Limitations:* Ssh is software and has vulnerabilities. The simplest way to subvert ssh is a "man in the middle" attack. Ssh will diagnose the attack, but most users ignore the "you may be under attack" warning and continue using the tool. Another way to subvert ssh is to compromise an authorized remote ssh endpoint or laptop.

signature-based intrusion-detection system – An intrusion-detection system with rules called "signatures" that identify suspicious behaviors for a computer, network or other system. The system raises alerts when the behavior of the system matches a rule. *Limitations:* Most intrusion-detection systems are software, and contain vulnerabilities that may be exploited. In addition, signatures are generally updated in signature-based systems only when new types of attacks come into widespread use. One common way to defeat signature-based intrusion-detection system is to steal credentials and log in remotely, rather than use traditional "attack" tools that match signatures. Another is to write new attack code or malware that does not match any existing signature.

SIS – See Safety Instrumented System.

spear-phishing – Phishing email designed with a particular individual in mind, generally reflecting information found on social media and other Internet sites.

ssh – See secure shell.

sneakernet – Carrying computers, USB drives and other machine-readable information past physical security boundaries into SCADA systems.

steganography – The study of hiding information in plain sight – for example, encoding an information stream in the low-order bits of pixel values in an image, thus changing the image to store information in ways that are imperceptible to a human eye.

Supervisory Control and Data Acquisition (SCADA) system – In popular usage, any industrial control system. In technical usage, any control system whose monitoring and/or control devices are spread throughout a wide-area network.

targeted, persistent attack – An attack by a persistent adversary, with a specific target, generally using interactive remote control techniques. Targeted attackers are unlikely to be distracted by other, less-well-defended targets, contradicting the common wisdom "you only need to be better defended than your neighbor."

TPA – See targeted, persistent attack.

trojan – Malicious software that claims to do some useful thing, but uses the computer running the trojan to carry out unauthorized activities as well.

two-factor authentication – Two factor authentication uses at least two different kinds of things to identify a user. Most commonly, these "things" are something the user knows, such as a password, and something else. The something else may be password-generation device, a finger print, or an iris scan. *Limitations:* Finger-print reader hardware and software has had vulnerabilities, as have other biometric scanners. Password-generation device master keys have been stolen. More fundamentally, two-factor authentication protects against attacks where an unknown attacker seeks to impersonate a legitimate user, but not against compromised endpoints. Malware that waits until two-factor authentication is complete before giving remote control of a compromised computer or remote access session to an attacker is not impaired by two-factor authentication.

unidirectional gateway – A combination of hardware physically able to transit information in only one direction, and software that replicates industrial servers and emulates industrial devices to external networks. Unidirectional gateways are deployed as cyber-perimeter protections between networks at different levels of criticality, most commonly between SCADA networks and IT networks, a WAN, or the Internet. *Limitations:* Unidirectional Gateways contain software, but for gateways oriented to transmit information out of protected SCADA systems, any software vulnerabilities are immaterial because of the protections the gateway hardware provides.

Universal Serial Bus – The communications system used to connect modern keyboards, mice, and removable storage drives to computers. *Limitations:* all USB devices contain CPUs and firmware, which can be subverted to attack connected computers. USB firmware can be very difficult to verify without physical damage to the USB device.

USB – See Universal Serial Bus.

virtual private network (VPN) – An encrypted connection between two endpoints. Endpoints may be computers or networks. A VPN transparently encrypts all communications between the endpoints, without communicating applications being aware that encryption is taking place. *Limitations:* Most VPNs are software and have vulnerabilities. If a VPN key is stolen, an unauthorized endpoint can impersonate an authorized endpoint. Compromised endpoints can communicate through a VPN – the VPN encrypts attacks as happily as it does legitimate communications.

virus – Malicious software that embeds copies of itself in existing files. When an application opens the infected file, it triggers execution of the embedded virus.

VPN – See virtual private network

vulnerability – A flaw that permits an adversary to make unauthorized use of a computing device. Known vulnerabilities are those both attackers and defenders are aware of. Unknown vulnerabilities are those neither attackers nor defenders are aware of yet. Zero-day vulnerabilities are those our attackers are aware of and are exploiting, but for which no antivirus, intrusion detection, security update or other specific remediation or compensating measure is available.

WAN – See wide-area network.

whitelisting – See application control.

white-box – Any artifact whose inner workings are evident to an external examiner. Common usage in security contexts is as an adjective applied to some sort of examination or test. Used this way, it means the examination or test starts with full access to information about how the system works internally. For example, a penetration test by a tester with full access to target and intermediate system, network and security designs. See also: black box.

wide-area network (WAN) – Any network that extends beyond the physical perimeter of an industrial site.

workstation – A computer used primarily to interact with a person, rather than with other computers. Contrast with server.

worm – Malicious software that launches copies of itself on other machines.

zero-day – A vulnerability for which no security update yet exists, and no antivirus or intrusion-detection signatures exist. Also: an exploit for such a vulnerability.

References

[1] K. Steenstrup, "IT and Operational Technology Alignment Innovation
     Key Initiative Overview," Gartner Group, 2014. [Online]. Available:
     https://www.gartner.com/doc/2691517/it-operational-technology-
     alignment-innovation#a-98481934.

[2] U.S. Chemical Safety and Hazard Investigation Board, "BP Texas City
     Refinery Explosion and Fire, Final Investigation Report," U.S. Chemical
     Safety and Hazard Investigation Board, 2007. [Online]. Available:
     http://www.csb.gov/assets/1/19/csbfinalreportbp.pdf.

[3] R. Langner, "To Kill a Centrifuge - A Technical Analysis of What
     Stuxnet's Creators Tried to Achieve," The Langner Group, 2013. [Online].
     Available: http://www.langner.com/en/wp-content/uploads/2013/11/To-
     kill-a-centrifguge.pdf.

[4] Bundesamt für Sicherheit in der Informationstechnik – BSI, "The State of
     IT Security in Germany 2014," Bundesamt für Sicherheit in der
     Informationstechnik – BSI, 2014. [Online]. Available:
     https://www.bsi.bund.de/SharedDocs/Downloads/EN/BSI/Publications/Se
     curitysituation/IT-Security-Situation-in-Germany-
     2014.pdf?__blob=publicationFile&v=3.

[5] R. M. Lee, M. Assante and T. Conway, "German Steel Mill Cyber
     Attack," SANS, 2014. [Online]. Available: http://ics.sans.org/media/ICS-
     CPPE-case-Study-2-German-Steelworks_Facility.pdf.

[6] DHS NCCOE ICS-CERT, "Alert IR-ALERT-H-16-056-01 Cyber-Attack
     Against Ukrainian Critical Infrastructure," U.S. Department of Homeland
     Security Industrial Control Systems Computer Emergency Response
     Team, 2016. [Online]. Available: https://ics-cert.us-cert.gov/alerts/IR-
     ALERT-H-16-056-01.

[7] Department of Homeland Security Control Systems Security Program,
     "Recommended Practice: Improving Industrial Control Systems
     Cybersecurity with Defense-In-Depth Strategies," 2009. [Online].
     Available: https://ics-cert.us-
     cert.gov/sites/default/files/recommended_practices/Defense_in_Depth_Oc
     t09.pdf.

[8] K. Stouffer, V. Pilliteri, S. Lightman, M. Abrams and A. Hahn, "NIST
     Special Publication 800-82 Revision 2, Guide to Industrial Control
     Systems (ICS) Security," Department of Commerce, National Institute of
     Standards and Technology, 2015. [Online]. Available: ,

http://nvlpubs.nist.gov/nistpubs/SpecialPublications/NIST.SP.800-82r2.pdf.

[9] National Security Agency Information Assurance Directorate, "Defense in Depth: A practical strategy for achieving Information Assurance in today's highly networked environments," 2010. [Online]. Available: https://www.iad.gov/iad/library/ia-guidance/archive/defense-in-depth.cfm.

[10] S. Kort, "The Security for Safety Problem in Cyberphysical Systems," Kaspersky Lab, 2015. [Online]. Available: http://mils-workshop.euromils.eu/downloads/hipeac_literature_2016/08-Kort_Ruina_MILSWorkshop2016.pdf.

[11] Industrial internet Consortium, "Industrial Internet Reference Architecture Version 1.7," 2015. [Online]. Available: http://www.iiconsortium.org/IIRA.htm.

[12] F. Artes, "The Targeted Persistent Attack (TPA) - When the Thing That Goes Bump in the Night Really is the Bogeyman," NSS Labs, 2012. [Online]. Available: https://www.nsslabs.com/blog/the-targeted-persistent-attack-tpa-when-the-thing-that-goes-bump-in-the-night-really-is-the-bogeyman/.

[13] S. Gallagher, "Two more healthcare networks caught up in outbreak of hospital ransomware," ArsTechnica, 2016. [Online]. Available: http://arstechnica.com/security/2016/03/two-more-healthcare-networks-caught-up-in-outbreak-of-hospital-ransomware.

[14] CBC News, "University of Calgary paid $20K in ransomware attack," 2016. [Online]. Available: http://www.cbc.ca/beta/news/canada/calgary/university-calgary-ransomware-cyberattack-1.3620979.

[15] Mandiant, "Mandiant APT1 - Exposing One of China's Cyber Espionage Units," 2013. [Online]. Available: http://intelreport.mandiant.com/Mandiant_APT1_Report.pdf.

[16] D. Alperovitch, "Revealed: Operation Shady RAT," McAfee, 2011. [Online]. Available: http://www.mcafee.com/us/resources/white-papers/wp-operation-shady-rat.pdf.

[17] The White House, "International Strategy for Cyberspace," 2011. [Online]. Available: http://whitehouse.gov/sites/defaultlfiles/rss_viewer/international_strategy_for_cyberspace.pdf.

[18] J. Leyden, "Hack on Saudi Aramco hit 30,000 workstations, oil firm admits," TheRegister, 2012. [Online]. Available:

http://www.theregister.co.uk/2012/08/29/saudi_aramco_malware_attack_a nalysis/.

[19] K. Zetter, "The NSA Acknowledges What We All Feared: Iran Learns From US Cyberattacks," Wired, 2015. [Online]. Available: https://www.wired.com/2015/02/nsa-acknowledges-feared-iran-learns-us-cyberattacks/.

[20] A. Ginter, "13 ways through a firewall: What you don't know can hurt you.," ISA Intech, 2013. [Online]. Available: https://www.isa.org/InTechTemplate.cfm?template=/ ContentManagement /ContentDisplay.cfm&ContentID=92916.

[21] Tripwire, "Tripwire Critical Infrastructure Study," 2015. [Online]. Available: http://www.tripwire.com/company/research/tripwire-critical-infrastructure-study.

[22] Ponemon Institute, "2016 Ponemon Cost of Data Breach Study," Ponemon Institute, 2016. [Online]. Available: http://www-3.ibm.com/security/data-breach.

[23] Nuclear Regulatory Commission, "Regulatory Guide 5.71: Cyber Security Programs for Nuclear Facilities," 2010. [Online]. Available: https://scp.nrc.gov/slo/regguide571.pdf.

[24] CSA Group, "N290.7-4 Cyber security for nuclear power plants and small reactor facilities," 2015. [Online]. Available: http://shop.csa.ca/en/canada/nuclear/n2907-14/invt/27037522014.

[25] Agence nationale de la sécurité des systèmes d'information (ANSSI), "Cybersecurity for Industrial Control Systems: Classification Method and Key Measures," 2014. [Online]. Available: http://www.ssi.gouv.fr/uploads/2014/01/industrial_security_WG_Classific ation_Method.pdf.

[26] Government of Canada, "Phishing, How many take the bait?," 2012. [Online]. Available: http://www.getcybersafe.gc.ca/cnt/rsrcs/nfgrphcs/nfgrphcs-2012-10-11-en.aspx.

[27] M. Bailey, "The Latest in Phishing: First of 2016," Wombat Security Technologies, 2016. [Online]. Available: https://info.wombatsecurity.com/blog/the-latest-in-phishing-first-of-2016.

[28] Symantec, "2016 Internet Security Threat Report," Symantec, 2016. [Online]. Available: https://www.symantec.com/content/dam/symantec/docs/reports/ istr-21-2016-en.pdf.

[29] B. Schneier, Secrets and Lies: Digital Security in a Networked World, Indianapolis: Wiley Publishing Inc., 2000.

[30] M. Waschke, How Clouds Hold IT Together: Integrating Architecture with Cloud Deployment, New York: Apress, 2015.

[31] A. Ginter, "No Silver Bullets - Whitelisting / Application Control," in *Proceedings of the SCADA Security Scientific Symposium 2012 (S4 Proceedings, Volume 6)*, Miami, 2012.

[32] North American Electric Reliability Corporation, "Critical Infrastructure Protection Standards Version 5," North American Electric Reliability Corporation, 2014. [Online]. Available: https://scadahacker.com/library/Documents/Standards/NERC%20-%20CIP%20v5%20Consolidated.pdf.

[33] D. Albright, P. Brannan and C. Walrond, "Stuxnet Malware and Natanz: Update of the ISIS December 22, 2010 Report," Institute for Science and International Security, 2011. [Online]. Available: http://isis-online.org/isis-reports/detail/stuxnet-malware-and-natanz-update-of-isis-december-22-2010-reportsupa-href1/8.

[34] N. Falliere, L. O. Murchu and E. Chien, "W32.Stuxnet.Dossier," Symantec, 2010. [Online]. Available: https://www.symantec.com/content/en/us/enterprise/media/security_response/whitepapers/w32_stuxnet_dossier.pdf.

[35] sKyWiper Analysis Team, Laboratory of Cryptography and System Security (CrySyS Lab) , "sKyWIper (a.k.a. Flame a.k.a. Flamer): A complex malware for targeted attacks, v1.05," 2012. [Online]. Available: http://www.crysys.hu/skywiper/skywiper.pdf.

[36] E. Byres, A. Ginter and J. Langill, "How Stuxnet Spreads – A Study of Infection Paths in Best Practice Systems," 2011. [Online]. Available: http://abterra.ca/papers/How-Stuxnet-Spreads.pdf.

[37] BIMCO, "The Guidelines On Cyber Security OnBoard Ships," 2016. [Online]. Available: http://www.ics-shipping.org/docs/default-source/resources/safety-security-and-operations/guidelines-on-cyber-security-onboard-ships.pdf?sfvrsn=12.

[38] Centre for the Protection of National Infrastructure, "Security For Industrial Control Systems Framework Overview," 2015. [Online]. Available: https://www.cpni.gov.uk/Documents/Publications/2016/SICS%20-%20Framework%20Overview%20Final%20v1%201.pdf.

[39] National Institute of Standards and Technology, "Framework For Improving Critical Infrastructure Cybersecurity," 2014. [Online]. Available: http://www.nist.gov/cyberframework/upload/cybersecurity-framework-021214.pdf.

[40] Office of Electricity Delivery and Energy Reliability, U.S. Department of Energy, "Cybersecurity Capability Maturity Model (C2M2)," 2014. [Online]. Available: http://energy.gov/sites/prod/files/2014/03/f13/C2M2-v1-1_cor.pdf.

[41] P. Feldman and D. Hill, "Cyber-risk, Standards and Best Practices," Electricity Policy, 2015. [Online]. Available: http://www.electricitypolicy.com/Articles/a-new-responsibility-for-utility-boards-of-directors-cybersecurity-2.

[42] National Institute of Standards and Technology, "NIST Special Publication 800-30 Revision 1, Guide for Conducting Risk Assessments," 2012. [Online]. Available: http://nvlpubs.nist.gov/nistpubs/Legacy/SP/nistspecialpublication800-30r1.pdf.

[43] D. Brooks and C. L. Smith, "Engineering Principles in the Protection of Assets," in *The Handbook of Security*, Palgrave MacMillan, 2014.

[44] A. Ginter, "Control System Security Attack Models," Cyber Security Review, 2015. [Online]. Available: http://www.cybersecurity-review.com/industry-perspective/control-system-security-attack-models.

[45] R. Langner, Robust Control System Networks, Momentum Press, 2011.

[46] B. Rolston, "Bow-Tying It All Together: Analyzing Your Attack Surface," OSIsoft, 2016. [Online]. Available: http://www.osisoft.com/Presentations/Bow-Tying-It-All-Together--Analyzing-Your-Attack-Surface/.

[47] North American Electric Reliability Corporation, "Guidance for Secure Interactive Remote Access," 2011. [Online]. Available: http://www.nerc.com/pa/rrm/bpsa/Alerts%20DL/2011%20Alerts/FINAL-Guidance_for_Secure_Interactive_Remote_Access.pdf.

[48] Center for the Protection of National Infrastructure, "Configuring & Managing Remote Access for Industrial Control Systems," Center for the Protection of National Infrastructure, 2011. [Online]. Available: http://www.cpni.gov.uk/documents/publications/2011/2011022-remote_access_for_ics_gpg.pdf?epslanguage=en-gb.

[49] Cisco Systems Inc. and Rockwell Automation Inc., "Achieving Secure, Remote Access to Plant-Floor Applications and Data," 2009. [Online].

Available:
https://scadahacker.com/library/Documents/ICS_Supplier_Reference/Roc
kwell%20-
%20Achieving%20Secure%20Remote%20Access%20(2009).pdf.

[50] McAfee, "Providing Secure Remote Access to Industrial Control Systems Using McAfee Firewall Enterprise (Sidewinder),," 2009. [Online]. Available:
https://kc.mcafee.com/resources/sites/MCAFEE/content/live/PRODUCT_
DOCUMENTATION/21000/PD21647/en_US/fe_7x_an_icsvpn_700-
2105A00_en-us.pdf.

[51] D. Peterson, "Chicken, Egg, and Chicken Omlet with Salsa," Digital Bond, 2013. [Online]. Available:
http://www.digitalbond.com/blog/2013/08/28/chicken-egg-and-chicken-
omelette-with-salsa/.

[52] D. Peterson, "PLC's: Insecure By Design v. Vulnerabilities," Digital Bond, 2011. [Online]. Available:
http://www.digitalbond.com/blog/2011/08/02/plcs-insecure-by-design-v-
vulnerabilities/, .

[53] D. Peterson, *personal communication,* 2016.

[54] Industrial Internet Consortium, "Industrial Internet Reference Architecture Version 1.7," 2015. [Online]. Available:
http://www.iiconsortium.org/IIRA.htm.

[55] Albrecht, Paterson and Watson, "Plaintext Recovery Attacks Against SSH," 2015. [Online]. Available:
http://www.isg.rhul.ac.uk/~kp/SandPfinal.pdf.

[56] M. Bellare, T. Kohno and C. Namprempre, "Authenticated encryption in SSH: provably fixing the SSH binary packet protocol," 2012. [Online]. Available: https://cseweb.ucsd.edu/~mihir/papers/ssh.pdf.

[57] T. Rid, "Cyber War Will Not Take Place," Journal of Strategic Studies, 2012. [Online]. Available:
http://dx.doi.org/10.1080/01402390.2011.608939.

[58] R. Johnson, "The IAEA Says It Has Inspectors At Iran's Fordo Nuclear Site And There Has Been No Explosion," Business Insider, 2013. [Online]. Available: http://www.businessinsider.com/massive-explosion-
reported-at-irans-fordow-nuclear-facility-2013-1.

About The Author

Andrew Ginter lives in Calgary, Alberta, Canada. He holds degrees in Applied Mathematics and Computer Science from the University of Calgary.

Andrew spent a decade developing SCADA software products for Daniel Computing Systems, Hewlett-Packard and Agilent Technologies. He spent half a decade developing IT/OT middleware products for Agilent Technologies and Verano. These products connected SCADA networks to IT networks, thereby contributing to the SCADA security problems that now plague the industry. This last decade Andrew spent as CTO and CSO at Industrial Defender, and then VP Industrial Security at Waterfall Security Solutions, working to develop, deploy and educate practitioners about industrial cyber-security products and technologies.

Andrew is the eldest of seven children born to German-speaking immigrants. He is married 28 years to a woman he adores, has two grown daughters of whom he is enormously proud, and teaches Tang Soo Do karate in his spare time.

Made in the USA
Lexington, KY
23 June 2017